This book is a must-read if…

- **You're a legal professional looking to hone your expertise in GDPR compliance.** This book breaks down the complex regulation into digestible pieces. No more trawling through legislative jargon – this book will save you time and elevate your understanding, helping you provide top-tier advice to your stakeholders in a language they understand.

- **You're a data protection professional navigating the nuanced world of data protection.** This guide goes beyond legalese, delving into real-world understanding and implications of GDPR. It's the one-stop resource to ensure you're at the forefront of privacy management and enhance your credibility.

- **You're just beginning your journey into the privacy profession.** This guide provides an accessible and comprehensive foundation. This book will kick-start your career, turning you from a novice into a knowledgeable pro in no time.

- **You're a business leader and have realised data protection is not just a 'legal issue'.** It's about trust and customer relationships. Understanding the GDPR is essential for leaders in today's digital world. This guide will help you shape an effective data privacy strategy, protect your company's reputation, and lead with confidence.

- **If you're an entrepreneur, coach or business owner.** Data privacy might seem like a 'big company' concern, but GDPR affects businesses of all sizes. This guide translates legal speak into clear, actionable steps, empowering you to protect your business and build customer trust. Say goodbye to the overwhelm – this guide makes GDPR compliance easy peasy!

Praise for The Easy Peasy Guide to the GDPR

"The GDPR was developed and put into effect for the purpose of protecting European citizens' data. While it lays out compliance requirements for data controllers and processors, it does so in a typical legalese-heavy fashion. *The Easy Peasy Guide* is an important effort made towards bridging the gap between the regulation and those it seeks to serve. Because of its accessibility and the value it adds to practitioners and non-practitioners alike, I will definitely be recommending this text in my classroom."

Matthew Lowe, Lecturer, University of Massachusetts Amherst, USA

———

"Effectively the CliffsNotes for GDPR, get the relevant points surfaced with a fraction of words, thus saving time. This is a very handy reference to keep nearby. You can quickly reference key talking points and not get lost in jargon."

Kevin Tunison, Data Protection Officer, UK

———

"*The Easy Peasy Guide* takes the complexity and legal jargon out of the GDPR and throws it out the window leaving you with an easy-to-understand guide for GDPR compliance."

Sharon Bauer, Founder, Bamboo Data Consulting, Canada

———

"*The Easy Peasy Guide to the GDPR* will leave its readers enriched with the necessary tools to interpret this regulation so that it can be meaningfully applied in their organisation."

Tripti Dhar, Partner, Reina Legal, India

"An incredibly useful tool to call upon when trying to navigate the complex maze of legal jargon that is the official GDPR text. By breaking the Articles down into plain English summaries, they become so much easier to comprehend!"

Jess Buj, Associate Director, Breakwater Solutions, Australia

―――

"*The Easy Peasy Guide* saves you time and helps simplify the GDPR during those high-pressure moments."

Alex Fetani, Senior Data Privacy Specialist, Fragomen, UK

―――

"I have had the privilege of reading the proposed changes to the UK GDPR from different commentators but I must say that your contribution is peerless. It is succinct, straight to the point, and easy to read. Not too long and not too short to lose its essence. Thank you.

I also find *The Easy Peasy Guide to the GDPR* very useful and insightful, as I prepare for my CIPP/E exam."

Emmanuel Omoju, Senior Manager, Tax Advisory, Regulatory and Data Privacy, Andersen, Nigeria

―――

"I want to thank you for sharing *The Easy Peasy Guide to the GDPR*. Very helpful and valuable."

Mohammed Shammout, GRC Senior Manager, PwC, Middle East

"For so many who find the text of the GDPR to be dense and complex, *The Easy Peasy Guide* will be a lifesaver that makes the law accessible."

Jules Polonetsky, CEO, Future of Privacy Forum, USA

———

"Such a great guide; very helpful to my understanding of the GDPR."

Kathleen Maloney, Senior Service Delivery Manager, Deloitte, USA

———

"I'm not familiar with GDPR, but just reading the first few of its Articles and your summaries of them, I can tell you've done a great job making reading the GDPR as easy as enjoying a cup of coffee with a piece of cake."

Sulan Bian, Senior Advisor – Privacy, Ministry of Business, Innovation and Employment, New Zealand

———

"The title *Easy Peasy Guide* doesn't do it justice. In the guide, you get a copy of the GDPR text broken into chapters. Jamal's guide is a plain English handy-dandy offline reference everyone should have on their device. While privacy pros can work magic, we can't always remember everything and with this guide, you don't need to."

Michael Thoreson, Founder, Krate Distributed Information Systems, Canada

———

"I found *The Easy Peasy Guide* the most simple, concise, jargon-less piece of work. I kept this guide as my handy tool to find quick references to GDPR. I highly recommend this guide for any practitioner looking to progress in the data protection career!"

Anisur Rahman, CEO, SMAR Alliance, UK

"Human-speak at its best – *The Easy Peasy Guide to the GDPR* is a must-have for one's repertoire! Whilst keeping the integrity of the official GDPR text, Jamal Ahmed provides a well-articulated summary under each Article of the GDPR. Whether new to the GDPR or getting back to basics, *The Easy Peasy Guide to the GDPR* is the optimal tool for anyone and everyone.

Thank you, Jamal Ahmed, the King of Data Protection, for fostering knowledge-sharing and growth amongst our communities at large."

Ayat Alihassan, Data Protection Program & Strategy, USA

———

"Jamal Ahmed has created an in-depth and accessible day-to-day real-life guide for businesses and practitioners to navigate the complexity of GDPR. It is difficult to make a complex subject easy to understand, but Jamal succeeds on all levels with *The Easy Peasy Guide to the GDPR*. I highly recommend the book as a great foundation for anyone wanting to understand GDPR."

Debbie Reynolds, CEO and Chief DPO, Debbie Reynolds Consulting, USA

———

"*The Easy Peasy Guide to the GDPR* is exactly that – Easy Peasy. But not in a bad way, in a I-can-finally-understand way. It's the ultimate reference for anyone who wants to get a clear understanding of what the GDPR actually says and not spend hours figuring out what was meant when reading the original."

Siobhan Solberg, Founder & Consultant, Raze, Greece

When I started my journey into the world of privacy,
I never could have imagined all that it would bring.

I am incredibly thankful for the unwavering support of my wife,
who has accompanied me on this journey every step of the way –
from taking risks to making sacrifices to build my career.
Her patience and understanding have been invaluable to me.

I'm also grateful for all the wonderful people I have met through
the Privacy Pros Network – those who have taken their time and put in
tremendous effort to educate themselves in data protection and privacy.

It's always amazing to be a part of such an inspiring and knowledgeable group.
This community is what makes privacy advocacy so valuable.

And finally, I want to express my deep gratitude towards my team at Kazient,
whose hard work and dedication has been instrumental in our progress.
Together, we are striving to make a real difference.

THE EASY PEASY GUIDE TO THE GDPR

GET CLARITY, GROW CONFIDENCE, AND GAIN CREDIBILITY

JAMAL AHMED GDPR (P) CIPP/E CIPM CIPT FIP

First published in Great Britain in 2023
by Book Brilliance Publishing
265A Fir Tree Road, Epsom, Surrey, KT17 3LF
+44 (0)20 8641 5090
www.bookbrilliancepublishing.com
admin@bookbrilliancepublishing.com

A CIP catalogue record for this book is available
at the British Library.

ISBN 978-1-913770-70-9

Typeset in Helvetica

CONTENTS

*"If you can't explain it simply,
you don't understand it well enough."*

– Albert Einstein

Introduction

The Easy Peasy Guide to the GDPR is the definitive resource for mastering the complexities of the General Data Protection Regulation (GDPR).

With my easy-to-understand format, you can quickly and confidently equip yourself with all the knowledge you need to protect your clients and business from non-compliance risks.

It's no secret that trying to make sense of the GDPR on your own can be overwhelming and intimidating. With its lengthy documents, legal jargon, and multiple layers required for protecting personal data, even experienced professionals struggle when it comes to getting up to speed with the GDPR. But that's why *The Easy Peasy Guide* is so important – it will help you understand the complexities of the GDPR in plain language so that you can explain it easily and effectively to colleagues, clients, or peers without resorting to robotic regurgitation of the Regulation.

For coaches, consultants, entrepreneurs, Chief Officers, as well as data protection, information governance and privacy professionals – this guide is an essential resource for demystifying EU data protection compliance Regulations.

As a coach or consultant, creating trust with your clients is essential for helping them reach their goals. Feeling uncertain about the requirements of the GDPR can make this difficult and leave you feeling just as frustrated as many other professionals in the same boat. Fortunately, this guide provides an easy-to-understand format which breaks down complicated legal jargon into straightforward steps to ensure compliance.

By investing time into reading this guide, you will be able to gain clarity on the GDPR without breaking a sweat – giving your clients peace of mind and avoiding any costly fines.

As an entrepreneur or business owner, the stress of understanding the GDPR and its effects on your business can be overwhelming. Not only are you worried about the potential reputational damage that comes with non-compliance, but also the effect it will have on losing the trust of customers and clients. If you're unable to demonstrate compliance, this could hinder your chances of acquiring new contracts from privacy-minded companies. I understand that a lot is at stake and hiring a data protection officer may not always be within reach.

That's why I created this guide – to provide you with clarity on the GDPR requirements for businesses as well as to help you confidently demonstrate compliance so that you can experience the true freedom of expanding your client portfolio. With this guide, implementing the GDPR does not have to be a daunting task; you can do it feeling safe in the knowledge that your data is protected!

As an Executive Officer, ensuring GDPR compliance for your organisation can be an intimidating task. With the threat of hefty fines and other penalties, it is crucial that you understand the Regulations and can effectively communicate them to staff.

This *Easy Peasy Guide* provides an invaluable resource for understanding and implementing GDPR compliance, helping you confidently lead your teams and protect your organisation from any potential risks. From gaining clarity on the GDPR requirements to communicating these Regulations to teams in a language they understand, this guide has everything you need – so you can lead with confidence knowing your data is protected.

The world of data privacy needs privacy professionals who have ultimate clarity on what the Regulation demands. Attaining industry certifications does not necessarily give you the confidence to implement and operationalise GDPR compliance. You may be feeling like an imposter, and struggle to explain it in a way your stakeholders can understand.

The Easy Peasy Guide will not only help you understand best practices in implementation, but will also give you the confidence to speak assertively on it so you can be the go-to person on GDPR compliance. Gain crystal clarity and take ultimate charge of data privacy – this guide will give you the power to approach GDPR compliance with confidence.

With a mission to empower organisations across the globe to protect their stakeholders' personal data, Kazient Privacy Experts has been providing comprehensive data protection guidance and training for businesses in over 137 countries.

Through Privacy Pros Academy, I have successfully trained high-performing professionals and enabled them to achieve International Association of Privacy Professionals (IAPP) certifications.

This book is the ultimate guide for fully comprehending the requirements of GDPR and mastering the art of data privacy.

Get started on your journey towards becoming a World-Class Privacy Professional with this essential guide – and help bring greater understanding of the GDPR requirements around the world.

PLEASE NOTE: This guide is not a replacement for the official text.

Rather, it breaks down the information in a way that is easy to digest, pulling on over 10 years of global experience as a leading Data Protection consultant and practitioner.

This is the guide I wish I had when I started my journey.

Thank you for taking the time to read and I look forward to connecting with you!

To your success,

Jamal Ahmed
CEO, Kazient Privacy Experts

1

General Provisions

Article 1

Subject Matter and Objectives

Official GDPR Text

1. This Regulation lays down rules relating to the protection of natural persons with regard to the processing of personal data and rules relating to the free movement of personal data.

2. This Regulation protects fundamental rights and freedoms of natural persons and in particular their right to the protection of personal data.

3. The free movement of personal data within the Union shall be neither restricted nor prohibited for reasons connected with the protection of natural persons with regard to the processing of personal data.

Easy Peasy Summary

This Regulation sets rules for the protection of people's personal data.

- This Regulation sets rules for the protection of people's personal data.

- These rules also cover the free movement of personal data.

- The rules protect the fundamental rights and freedoms of people's personal data.

- Personal data should not be limited or stopped from moving freely within the European Union, for the purpose of protecting personal data.

Article 2

Material Scope and Expectations

Official GDPR Text

1. This Regulation applies to the processing of personal data wholly or partly by automated means and to the processing other than by automated means of personal data which form part of a filing system or are intended to form part of a filing system.

2. This Regulation does not apply to the processing of personal data:

   a. in the course of an activity which falls outside the scope of Union law;

   b. by the Member States when carrying out activities which fall within the scope of Chapter 2 of Title V of the TEU;

   c. by a natural person in the course of a purely personal or household activity;

   d. by competent authorities for the purposes of the prevention, investigation, detection or prosecution of criminal offences or the execution of criminal penalties, including the safeguarding against and the prevention of threats to public security.

3. For the processing of personal data by the Union institutions, bodies, offices and agencies, Regulation (EC) No 45/2001 applies. Regulation (EC) No 45/2001 and other Union legal acts applicable to such processing of personal data shall be adapted to the principles and rules of this Regulation in accordance with Article 98.

4. This Regulation shall be without prejudice to the application of Directive 2000/31/EC, in particular of the liability rules of intermediary service providers in Articles 12 to 15 of that Directive.

Easy Peasy Summary

The rules apply where the personal data is processed manually if it's part of a filing system.

- The rules apply where the processing of personal data involves electronic processing.

- The rules apply where the personal data is processed manually if it's part of a filing system.

- The rules **do not** apply where:

  - the processing is outside the scope of Union law;

  - activities fall under Chapter 2 of Title V of the Treaty on the European Union;

  - someone is using the personal data for personal or household activities;

  - competent authorities are performing duties as required by law to prevent, investigate or detect crimes and uphold public safety and security.

Article 3
Territorial Scope

1

Official GDPR Text

1. This Regulation applies to the processing of personal data in the context of the activities of an establishment of a controller or a processor in the Union, regardless of whether the processing takes place in the Union or not.

2. This Regulation applies to the processing of personal data of data subjects who are in the Union by a controller or processor not established in the Union, where the processing activities are related to:

   a. the offering of goods or services, irrespective of whether a payment of the data subject is required, to such data subjects in the Union; or

   b. the monitoring of their behaviour as far as their behaviour takes place within the Union.

3. This Regulation applies to the processing of personal data by a controller not established in the Union, but in a place where Member State law applies by virtue of public international law.

Easy Peasy Summary

- The Regulation applies to the processing of personal data by controllers and processors within the European Union (EU or Union), regardless of whether the processing takes place inside or outside the EU.

- The Regulation applies when a company based outside of the European Union is processing personal data relating to people in the EU when:

- offering goods or services to people living in the European Union, whether or not they have to pay for it, or;

- the behaviour of people in the European Union is being monitored.

- This Regulation applies to the processing of personal data by a controller who is not based in the European Union, but who processes personal data in a place where European Union law applies (due to public international law, such as an embassy or a ship).

Article 4

Definitions

Official GDPR Text

For the purposes of this Regulation:

1. '**personal data**' means any information relating to an identified or identifiable natural person ('data subject'); an identifiable natural person is one who can be identified, directly or indirectly, in particular by reference to an identifier such as a name, an identification number, location data, an online identifier or to one or more factors specific to the physical, physiological, genetic, mental, economic, cultural or social identity of that natural person;

   'personal data' means any information relating to an identified or identifiable natural person ('data subject')

2. '**processing**' means any operation or set of operations which is performed on personal data or on sets of personal data, whether or not by automated means, such as collection, recording, organisation, structuring, storage, adaptation or alteration, retrieval, consultation, use, disclosure by transmission, dissemination or otherwise making available, alignment or combination, restriction, erasure or destruction;

3. '**restriction of processing**' means the marking of stored personal data with the aim of limiting their processing in the future;

4. '**profiling**' means any form of automated processing of personal data consisting of the use of personal data to evaluate certain personal aspects relating to a natural person, in particular to analyse or predict aspects concerning that natural person's performance at work, economic situation, health, personal preferences, interests, reliability, behaviour, location or movements;

5. '**pseudonymisation**' means the processing of personal data in such a manner that the personal data can no longer be attributed to a specific data subject without the use of additional information, provided that such additional information is kept separately and is subject to technical and organisational measures to ensure that the personal data are not attributed to an identified or identifiable natural person;

'filing system' means any structured set of personal data which are accessible according to specific criteria...

6. '**filing system**' means any structured set of personal data which are accessible according to specific criteria, whether centralised, decentralised or dispersed on a functional or geographical basis;

7. '**controller**' means the natural or legal person, public authority, agency or other body which, alone or jointly with others, determines the purposes and means of the processing of personal data; where the purposes and means of such processing are determined by Union or Member State law, the controller or the specific criteria for its nomination may be provided for by Union or Member State law;

8. '**processor**' means a natural or legal person, public authority, agency or other body which processes personal data on behalf of the controller;

9. '**recipient**' means a natural or legal person, public authority, agency or another body, to which the personal data are disclosed, whether a third party or not. However, public authorities which may receive personal data in the framework of a particular inquiry in accordance with Union or Member State law shall not be regarded as recipients; the processing of those data by those public authorities shall be in compliance with the applicable data protection rules according to the purposes of the processing;

10. '**third party**' means a natural or legal person, public authority, agency or body other than the data subject, controller, processor and persons who, under the direct authority of the controller or processor, are authorised to process personal data;

11. '**consent**' of the data subject means any freely given, specific, informed and unambiguous indication of the data subject's wishes by which he or she, by a statement or by a clear affirmative action, signifies agreement to the processing of personal data relating to him or her;

12. '**personal data breach**' means a breach of security leading to the accidental or unlawful destruction, loss, alteration, unauthorised disclosure of, or access to, personal data transmitted, stored or otherwise processed;

13. '**genetic data**' means personal data relating to the inherited or acquired genetic characteristics of a natural person which give unique information about the physiology or the health of that natural person and which result, in particular, from an analysis of a biological sample from the natural person in question;

14. '**biometric data**' means personal data resulting from specific technical processing relating to the physical, physiological or behavioural characteristics of a natural person, which allow or confirm the unique identification of that natural person, such as facial images or dactyloscopic data;

15. '**data concerning health**' means personal data related to the physical or mental health of a natural person, including the provision of health care services, which reveal information about his or her health status;

16. '**main establishment**' means:

   a. as regards a controller with establishments in more than one Member State, the place of its central administration in the Union, unless the decisions on the purposes and means of the processing of personal data are taken in another establishment of the controller in the Union and the latter establishment has the power to have such decisions implemented, in which case the establishment having taken such decisions is to be considered to be the main establishment;

   b. as regards a processor with establishments in more than one Member State, the place of its central administration in the Union, or, if the processor has no central administration in the Union, the establishment of the processor in the Union where the main processing activities in the context of the activities of an establishment of the processor take place to the extent that the processor is subject to specific obligations under this Regulation;

17. '**representative**' means a natural or legal person established in the Union who, designated by the controller or processor in writing pursuant to Article 27, represents the controller or processor with regard to their respective obligations under this Regulation;

18. '**enterprise**' means a natural or legal person engaged in an economic activity, irrespective of its legal form, including partnerships or associations regularly engaged in an economic activity;

19. '**group of undertakings**' means a controlling undertaking and its controlled undertakings;

20. '**binding corporate rules**' means personal data protection policies which are adhered to by a controller or processor established on the territory of a Member State for transfers or a set of transfers of personal data to a controller or processor in one or more third countries within a group of undertakings, or group of enterprises engaged in a joint economic activity;

21. '**supervisory authority**' means an independent public authority which is established by a Member State pursuant to Article 51;

22. '**supervisory authority concerned**' means a supervisory authority which is concerned by the processing of personal data because:

   a. the controller or processor is established on the territory of the Member State of that supervisory authority;

   b. data subjects residing in the Member State of that supervisory authority are substantially affected or likely to be substantially affected by the processing; or

   c. a complaint has been lodged with that supervisory authority;

23. '**cross-border processing**' means either:

   a. processing of personal data which takes place in the context of the activities of establishments in more than one Member State of a controller or processor in the Union where the controller or processor is established in more than one Member State; or

   b. processing of personal data which takes place in the context of the activities of a single establishment of a controller or processor in the Union but which substantially affects or is likely to substantially affect data subjects in more than one Member State.

24. **'relevant and reasoned objection'** means an objection to a draft decision as to whether there is an infringement of this Regulation, or whether envisaged action in relation to the controller or processor complies with this Regulation, which clearly demonstrates the significance of the risks posed by the draft decision as regards the fundamental rights and freedoms of data subjects and, where applicable, the free flow of personal data within the Union;

25. **'information society service'** means a service as defined in point (b) of Article 1(1) of Directive (EU) 2015/1535 of the European Parliament and of the Council (¹);

26. **'international organisation'** means an organisation and its subordinate bodies governed by public international law, or any other body which is set up by, or on the basis of, an agreement between two or more countries.

Easy Peasy Summary

'personal data' is any information about someone ... that can uniquely identify them ...

This Regulation has 26 key words. Here is what they mean:

- **'personal data'** is any information about someone (the 'data subject') that can uniquely identify them (such as their name, Social Security or National Insurance number, email address, photo etc. and/or things such as physical characteristics, health status, genetic makeup, mental state, economic situation, cultural background or social identity).

- **'processing'** is anything that is done to or with personal data or sets of personal data, whether manually or electronically. This includes collecting, recording, organising, structuring, storing, adapting or altering, retrieving, consulting, using, disclosing by transmission, disseminating or otherwise making available, aligning or combining, restricting, erasing or destroying the data.

- 'restriction of processing' is the setting aside of that person's personal data so it is no longer processed going forward.

- 'profiling' is processing of personal data using a machine to analyse or make predictions on personal aspects about someone, like how they might work, how healthy they are, what their interests are, etc.

- 'pseudonymisation' is masking personal data in a way that it cannot be linked to any specific person without extra information. This extra information must be kept separately and securely, so that it cannot unmask the personal data back to any person whom the personal data relates to.

- a 'filing system' is anything that stores personal data in an organised way. The personal data can be found by specific criteria, whether it is centrally located, decentralised or spread out over different areas, such as by surname or date, a particular box or shelf, a file or folder, etc.

- a 'controller' is any person or organisation who makes decisions about why and how personal data is processed. This could be an individual or a legal person as a limited company, a partnership, a publicly listed company, an association, public authority, agency, etc.

- a 'processor' is any person or organisation that does something with personal data because a controller has given them instructions to do so.

- a 'recipient' is the person or organisation who receives personal data, regardless of whether they are a third party.

- a 'third party' is any person or organisation who is directly authorised by a controller or processor to process personal data (but is not the data subject, the controller or the processor themselves).

'profiling' is processing of personal data using a machine to analyse or make predictions ...

- **'consent'** is a statement or action that shows the data subject gives permission for their personal data to be processed. The permission must be freely given, clear, concise, specific, and not based on silence or inaction.

- a **'personal data breach'** is when an unauthorised person or organisation either destroys, loses, alters, discloses or accesses personal data because of a security issue.

- **'genetic data'** is personal data that is related to a someone's genes. This can include information about their health and what they inherited from their parents. Genetic data is collected by analysing a biological sample from them.

- **'biometric data'** is personal data that is collected using specific technical methods to identify someone's physical, physiological or behavioural characteristics. This includes fingerprints, facial print, someone's gait, voice, iris scan, palm print, etc.

- **'data concerning health'** is any information about someone's physical or mental health, including information about any health care services they have received.

... the 'main establishment' for controllers, is the place where the headquarters are based.

- the **'main establishment'**

  o for controllers, is the place where the headquarters are based. However, if decisions about how personal data is processed is decided in another place, then that other place will be considered the main establishment.

  o for processors, it is the place where the headquarters are based. However, if the headquarters are not based in the European Union, then it means the place where the processing takes place, as long as the processor is required to follow some of the rules of this Regulation.

- a '**representative**' is the person or organisation that the controller or processor has arranged to act on their behalf within the European Union with regards to their obligations under this Regulation.

- an '**enterprise**' is a person or company that does business, including partnerships and groups that do business together regularly.

- a '**group of undertakings**' is where a company has other businesses that it controls through financial ownership of a company's capital, or through controlling the majority of votes in a company, or through naming more than 50% of the company's administrative, management or supervisory body.

- '**binding corporate rules**' means that a controller or processor that is established in the European Union has a set of policy documents that everyone in the organisation will follow. This allows them to send and access personal data by any person in any office anywhere in the world.

- a '**supervisory authority**' is an independent public authority which has been established by a Member State.

- a '**supervisory authority concerned**' means a supervisory authority which is interested in the processing of personal data because:

  - the controller or processor is established in the place of that supervisory authority;

  - people who live in the place where the supervisory authority is based are greatly affected, or;

  - a complaint has been lodged with that supervisory authority.

- 'cross-border processing' is where either;

  o a controller or processor processes personal data in places in more than one Member State, or;

  o a controller or processor processes personal data in one place but the processing greatly affects data subjects that live in other Member States.

- a 'relevant and reasoned objection' means an objection to a draft decision about whether there is an infringement of this Regulation, or whether planned action related to the controller or processor follows this Regulation. This type of objection should clearly demonstrate how the risks posed by the draft decision has an impact on fundamental rights and freedoms of data subjects, as well as the free flow of personal data within the European Union.

- 'information society service' means a service as defined in point (b) of Article 1(1) of Directive (EU) 2015/1535 of the European Parliament and of the Council (¹).

- an 'international organisation' is any organisation that is governed by public international law (including its subordinate bodies), or any other organisation that has been set up by more than one country by some sort of agreement.

2

Principles

Article 5

Principles Relating to Processing of Personal Data

Official GDPR Text

1. Personal data shall be:

   a. processed lawfully, fairly and in a transparent manner in relation to the data subject ('<u>lawfulness, fairness and transparency</u>');

   b. collected for specified, explicit and legitimate purposes and not further processed in a manner that is incompatible with those purposes; further processing for archiving purposes in the public interest, scientific or historical research purposes or statistical purposes shall, in accordance with Article 89(1), not be considered to be incompatible with the initial purposes ('<u>purpose limitation</u>');

   ... adequate, relevant and limited to what is necessary ...

   c. adequate, relevant and limited to what is necessary in relation to the purposes for which they are processed ('<u>data minimisation</u>');

   d. accurate and, where necessary, kept up to date; every reasonable step must be taken to ensure that personal data that are inaccurate, having regard to the purposes for which they are processed, are erased or rectified without delay ('<u>accuracy</u>');

   e. kept in a form which permits identification of data subjects for no longer than is necessary for the purposes for which the personal data are processed; personal data may be stored for longer periods insofar as the personal data will be processed solely for archiving purposes in the public interest, scientific or historical research purposes or statistical purposes in accordance with Article 89(1)

2

subject to implementation of the appropriate technical and organisational measures required by this Regulation in order to safeguard the rights and freedoms of the data subject ('<u>storage limitation</u>');

f. processed in a manner that ensures appropriate security of the personal data, including protection against unauthorised or unlawful processing and against accidental loss, destruction or damage, using appropriate technical or organisational measures ('<u>integrity and confidentiality</u>').

2. The controller shall be responsible for, and be able to demonstrate compliance with, paragraph 1 ('<u>accountability</u>').

Easy Peasy Summary

- Personal data must be processed lawfully, fairly, and in an open manner ('<u>lawfulness, fairness and transparency</u>').

- It must be collected for specific, explicit and approved reasons. If the personal data is to be used for other reasons, it must be processed in a way that does not go against the original purposes. However, further processing for archiving in the public interest, scientific research, or statistical research is allowed ('<u>purpose limitation</u>').

- Personal data must be sufficient for its intended purpose. It should be directly related to the purpose it is being collected for. It should be limited to what is required to meet the desired goal ('<u>data minimisation</u>').

- Personal data must be accurate and up to date. Controllers must take reasonable steps to ensure that inaccurate personal data are erased or corrected as soon as possible ('<u>accuracy</u>').

Personal data must be processed lawfully, fairly, and in an open manner ...

- Personal data should be kept in a way that lets us identify the people involved for only as long as required ('storage limitation').

Personal data must be processed safely and securely.

- Personal data must be processed safely and securely. It must be protected from unauthorised or unlawful processing and accidental loss, destruction, or damage. This should be done by using appropriate technical or organisational/ administrative measures ('integrity and confidentiality').

- The controller is responsible for complying with the principles. They should be able to prove such compliance ('accountability').

Article 6
Lawfulness of Processing

Official GDPR Text

1. Processing shall be lawful only if and to the extent that at least one of the following applies:

   a. the data subject has given consent to the processing of his or her personal data for one or more specific purposes;

   b. processing is necessary for the performance of a contract to which the data subject is party or in order to take steps at the request of the data subject prior to entering into a contract;

   c. processing is necessary for compliance with a legal obligation to which the controller is subject;

   d. processing is necessary in order to protect the vital interests of the data subject or of another natural person;

   e. processing is necessary for the performance of a task carried out in the public interest or in the exercise of official authority vested in the controller;

   f. processing is necessary for the purposes of the legitimate interests pursued by the controller or by a third party, except where such interests are overridden by the interests or fundamental rights and freedoms of the data subject which require protection of personal data, in particular where the data subject is a child.

2. Point (f) of the first subparagraph shall not apply to processing carried out by public authorities in the performance of their tasks.

3. Member States may maintain or introduce more specific provisions to adapt the application of the rules of this Regulation with regard to processing for compliance with points (c) and (e) of paragraph 1 by determining more precisely specific requirements for the processing and other measures to ensure lawful and fair processing, including for other specific processing situations as provided for in Chapter IX.

4. The basis for the processing referred to in point (c) and (e) of paragraph 1 shall be laid down by:

   a. Union law; or

   b. Member State law to which the controller is subject.

5. The purpose of the processing shall be determined in that legal basis or, as regards the processing referred to in point (e) of paragraph 1, shall be necessary for the performance of a task carried out in the public interest or in the exercise of official authority vested in the controller. That legal basis may contain specific provisions to adapt the application of rules of this Regulation, inter alia: the general conditions governing the lawfulness of processing by the controller; the types of data which are subject to the processing; the data subjects concerned; the entities to, and the purposes for which, the personal data may be disclosed; the purpose limitation; storage periods; and processing operations and processing procedures, including measures to ensure lawful and fair processing such as those for other specific processing situations as provided for in Chapter IX. The Union or the Member State law shall meet an objective of public interest and be proportionate to the legitimate aim pursued.

2

6. Where the processing for a purpose other than that for which the personal data have been collected is not based on the data subject's consent or on a Union or Member State law which constitutes a necessary and proportionate measure in a democratic society to safeguard the objectives referred to in Article 23(1), the controller shall, in order to ascertain whether processing for another purpose is compatible with the purpose for which the personal data are initially collected, take into account, inter alia:

   a. any link between the purposes for which the personal data have been collected and the purposes of the intended further processing;

   b. the context in which the personal data have been collected, in particular regarding the relationship between data subjects and the controller;

   c. the nature of the personal data, in particular whether special categories of personal data are processed, pursuant to Article 9, or whether personal data related to criminal convictions and offences are processed, pursuant to Article 10;

   d. the possible consequences of the intended further processing for data subjects;

   e. the existence of appropriate safeguards, which may include encryption or pseudonymisation.

Easy Peasy Summary

*Controllers
must have
consent from
the data
subject ...*

- For processing of personal data to be lawful:

  - controllers must have consent from the data subject, or;

  - processing is required to get into a contract or perform a contract, or;

  - processing is required to comply with a law or Regulation, or;

  - processing is required to keep someone alive, or;

  - processing is required in the interests of the public or to carry out some official duty, or;

  - processing is required for your or a third party's interests (provided it does not flout on the data subject's rights and freedoms).

- Public authorities – including government agencies, some administrative offices and teaching services – cannot rely on legitimate interests to carry out their tasks.

- Member States can make specific rules to adapt how the rules of this Regulation are applied when it comes to processing, and that it is done to ensure compliance with points (c) and (e) above.

- This includes making specific requirements for processing and taking other measures to ensure lawful and fair processing in other specific situations, as set out in Chapter IX.

- Either Union law or Member State law will set out the type of processing that is a legal obligation and in the public interest.

- If a controller want to process personal data for a reason other than the original reason it was collected for, then the controller needs to check if that is compatible with their original purpose, by considering:

- o the link between the original reason and the new reason;

- o the relationship between the controller and the data subject and how this information was collected;

- o the type of personal data they want to process (and whether it is special category or related to criminal convictions and offences);

- o how this might affect the data subject(s);

- o what measures they are taking to keep the personal data secure and private.

2

Article 7

Conditions for Consent

Official GDPR Text

1. Where processing is based on consent, the controller shall be able to demonstrate that the data subject has consented to processing of his or her personal data.

2. If the data subject's consent is given in the context of a written declaration which also concerns other matters, the request for consent shall be presented in a manner which is clearly distinguishable from the other matters, in an intelligible and easily accessible form, using clear and plain language. Any part of such a declaration which constitutes an infringement of this Regulation shall not be binding.

3. The data subject shall have the right to withdraw his or her consent at any time. The withdrawal of consent shall not affect the lawfulness of processing based on consent before its withdrawal. Prior to giving consent, the data subject shall be informed thereof. It shall be as easy to withdraw as to give consent.

4. When assessing whether consent is freely given, utmost account shall be taken of whether, inter alia, the performance of a contract, including the provision of a service, is conditional on consent to the processing of personal data that is not necessary for the performance of that contract.

Easy Peasy Summary

- The controller must show that the data subject has given consent.

- Consent wording must be clear, concise and in plain language. It should be provided separately from any other information, and it must be easy to access.

- The data subject should be able to withdraw their consent any time and do so just as easily as they gave it.

- The consent wording should be specific to each purpose.

- The consent should be freely given – there should be no imbalance of power, and there should be no detriment if someone does not give consent.

- Consent should not be a condition of accessing a service.

Article 8

Conditions Applicable to Child's Consent in Relation to Information Society Services

Official GDPR Text

1. Where point (a) of Article 6(1) applies, in relation to the offer of information society services directly to a child, the processing of the personal data of a child shall be lawful where the child is at least 16 years old. Where the child is below the age of 16 years, such processing shall be lawful only if and to the extent that consent is given or authorised by the holder of parental responsibility over the child. Member States may provide by law for a lower age for those purposes provided that such lower age is not below 13 years.

2. The controller shall make reasonable efforts to verify in such cases that consent is given or authorised by the holder of parental responsibility over the child, taking into consideration available technology.

3. Paragraph 1 shall not affect the general contract law of Member States such as the rules on the validity, formation or effect of a contract in relation to a child.

Easy Peasy Summary

Only someone who is 16 years or older can give consent.

- Only someone who is 16 years or older can give consent.

- If someone is under 16 years old, then a parent or guardian must provide consent.

- Member States have the power to lower the age of consent, but not below 13 years old.

- Controllers should make reasonable efforts to be sure consent has actually been given by the parent or guardian.

- Contract law of any Member State will not be affected by this requirement.

2

Article 9

Processing of Special Categories of Personal Data

Official GDPR Text

1. Processing of personal data revealing racial or ethnic origin, political opinions, religious or philosophical beliefs, or trade union membership, and the processing of genetic data, biometric data for the purpose of uniquely identifying a natural person, data concerning health or data concerning a natural person's sex life or sexual orientation shall be prohibited.

2. Paragraph 1 shall not apply if one of the following applies:

   a. the data subject has given explicit consent to the processing of those personal data for one or more specified purposes, except where Union or Member State law provide that the prohibition referred to in paragraph 1 may not be lifted by the data subject;

   b. processing is necessary for the purposes of carrying out the obligations and exercising specific rights of the controller or of the data subject in the field of employment and social security and social protection law in so far as it is authorised by Union or Member State law or a collective agreement pursuant to Member State law providing for appropriate safeguards for the fundamental rights and the interests of the data subject;

   c. processing is necessary to protect the vital interests of the data subject or of another natural person where the data subject is physically or legally incapable of giving consent;

2

d. processing is carried out in the course of its legitimate activities with appropriate safeguards by a foundation, association or any other not-for-profit body with a political, philosophical, religious or trade union aim and on condition that the processing relates solely to the members or to former members of the body or to persons who have regular contact with it in connection with its purposes and that the personal data are not disclosed outside that body without the consent of the data subjects;

e. processing relates to personal data which are manifestly made public by the data subject;

f. processing is necessary for the establishment, exercise or defence of legal claims or whenever courts are acting in their judicial capacity;

g. processing is necessary for reasons of substantial public interest, on the basis of Union or Member State law which shall be proportionate to the aim pursued, respect the essence of the right to data protection and provide for suitable and specific measures to safeguard the fundamental rights and the interests of the data subject;

h. processing is necessary for the purposes of preventive or occupational medicine, for the assessment of the working capacity of the employee, medical diagnosis, the provision of health or social care or treatment or the management of health or social care systems and services on the basis of Union or Member State law or pursuant to contract with a health professional and subject to the conditions and safeguards referred to in paragraph 3;

... processing relates to personal data which are manifestly made public by the data subject ...

i. processing is necessary for reasons of public interest in the area of public health, such as protecting against serious cross-border threats to health or ensuring high standards of quality and safety of health care and of medicinal products or medical devices, on the basis of Union or Member State law which provides for suitable and specific measures to safeguard the rights and freedoms of the data subject, in particular professional secrecy;

j. processing is necessary for archiving purposes in the public interest, scientific or historical research purposes or statistical purposes in accordance with Article 89(1) based on Union or Member State law which shall be proportionate to the aim pursued, respect the essence of the right to data protection and provide for suitable and specific measures to safeguard the fundamental rights and the interests of the data subject.

3. Personal data referred to in paragraph 1 may be processed for the purposes referred to in point (h) of paragraph 2 when those data are processed by or under the responsibility of a professional subject to the obligation of professional secrecy under Union or Member State law or rules established by national competent bodies or by another person also subject to an obligation of secrecy under Union or Member State law or rules established by national competent bodies.

4. Member States may maintain or introduce further conditions, including limitations, with regard to the processing of genetic data, biometric data or data concerning health.

Easy Peasy Summary

- Controllers must not process personal data that shows someone's:

  o racial or ethnic origin;

  o political opinions;

  o religious or philosophical beliefs;

  o trade union membership;

  o genetic data;

  o biometric data;

  o health data;

  o sexual life; or

  o sexual orientation.

- But controllers can process special category personal data where they can rely on one of the following conditions:

  o the data subject has given explicit consent;

  o processing is in context of employment, social security or social protection law;

  o to keep a person alive where they cannot physically or legally give consent;

  o processing is done by an organisation with a political, philosophical, religious or trade union purpose of its members such as a church;

  o the data subject has made this personal data public already, such as by posting on social media, during a TV or radio interview, or writing about it in a book;

- if it is necessary to make or defend some sort of legal claim;

- processing is necessary in the interests of the public based on Member State or Union law;

- it is necessary for preventive or occupational medicine, to assess the working capacity of the employee, medical diagnosis, the provision of health or social care or treatment or the management of health or social care systems;

- processing is required in the interests of public health;

- it is necessary for public archives, scientific or historical research, or statistical purposes.

Article 10

Processing of Personal Data Related to Criminal Convictions and Offences

2

Official GDPR Text

Processing of personal data relating to criminal convictions and offences or related security measures based on Article 6(1) shall be carried out only under the control of official authority or when the processing is authorised by Union or Member State law providing for appropriate safeguards for the rights and freedoms of data subjects. Any comprehensive register of criminal convictions shall be kept only under the control of official authority.

Easy Peasy Summary

- Personal data about convictions or offences can only be processed:

  o   under the control of official authority; or

  o   when Union or Member State law authorises the processing.

- The processing must be done safely and securely.

- Only an official authority can keep a register of criminal convictions.

Only an official authority can keep a register of criminal convictions.

Article 11

Processing Which Does Not Require Identification

Official GDPR Text

1. If the purposes for which a controller processes personal data do not or do no longer require the identification of a data subject by the controller, the controller shall not be obliged to maintain, acquire or process additional information in order to identify the data subject for the sole purpose of complying with this Regulation.

2. Where, in cases referred to in paragraph 1 of this Article, the controller is able to demonstrate that it is not in a position to identify the data subject, the controller shall inform the data subject accordingly, if possible. In such cases, Articles 15 to 20 shall not apply except where the data subject, for the purpose of exercising his or her rights under those articles, provides additional information enabling his or her identification.

Easy Peasy Summary

If a controller cannot identify a data subject, they must tell the data subject.

- A controller is not required to maintain, get, or process more information to identify the data subject if the controller does not need to anymore, just to be able to comply with this Regulation.

- If a controller cannot identify a data subject, they must tell the data subject. If the data subject wants to access their rights, they need to provide more information so the controller can be sure they are who they say they are.

3

Rights of the Subject Data

Article 12

Transparent Information, Communication and Modalities for the Exercise of the Rights of the Data Subject

Official GDPR Text

1. The controller shall take appropriate measures to provide any information referred to in Articles 13 and 14 and any communication under Articles 15 to 22 and 34 relating to processing to the data subject in a concise, transparent, intelligible and easily accessible form, using clear and plain language, in particular for any information addressed specifically to a child. The information shall be provided in writing, or by other means, including, where appropriate, by electronic means. When requested by the data subject, the information may be provided orally, provided that the identity of the data subject is proven by other means.

2. The controller shall facilitate the exercise of data subject rights under Articles 15 to 22. In the cases referred to in Article 11(2), the controller shall not refuse to act on the request of the data subject for exercising his or her rights under Articles 15 to 22, unless the controller demonstrates that it is not in a position to identify the data subject.

3. The controller shall provide information on action taken on a request under Articles 15 to 22 to the data subject without undue delay and in any event within one month of receipt of the request. That period may be extended by two further months where necessary, taking into account the complexity and number of the requests. The controller shall inform the data subject of any such extension within one month of receipt of the request, together with the reasons for the delay. Where the data subject makes the request by electronic form means, the information shall be provided by electronic means where possible, unless otherwise requested by the data subject.

4. If the controller does not take action on the request of the data subject, the controller shall inform the data subject without delay and at the latest within one month of receipt of the request of the reasons for not taking action and on the possibility of lodging a complaint with a supervisory authority and seeking a judicial remedy.

5. Information provided under Articles 13 and 14 and any communication and any actions taken under Articles 15 to 22 and 34 shall be provided free of charge. Where requests from a data subject are manifestly unfounded or excessive, in particular because of their repetitive character, the controller may either:

   a. charge a reasonable fee taking into account the administrative costs of providing the information or communication or taking the action requested; or

   b. refuse to act on the request.

   The controller shall bear the burden of demonstrating the manifestly unfounded or excessive character of the request.

6. Without prejudice to Article 11, where the controller has reasonable doubts concerning the identity of the natural person making the request referred to in Articles 15 to 21, the controller may request the provision of additional information necessary to confirm the identity of the data subject.

7. The information to be provided to data subjects pursuant to Articles 13 and 14 may be provided in combination with standardised icons in order to give in an easily visible, intelligible and clearly legible manner a meaningful overview of the intended processing. Where the icons are presented electronically they shall be machine-readable.

8. The Commission shall be empowered to adopt delegated acts in accordance with Article 92 for the purpose of determining the information to be presented by the icons and the procedures for providing standardised icons.

3

Easy Peasy Summary

- Controllers need to make sure data subjects get information about their data subject rights.

- This information must be clear and easy to understand, especially when it concerns children.

- The information must be presented in a way that is easy for the data subject to understand, whether it is written, oral, or electronic.

The controller is responsible for helping people exercise their data subject rights.

- The controller is responsible for helping people exercise their data subject rights. If the person requesting help is known to the controller, they must comply with the request. If the controller cannot identify the person, they can refuse to help.

- The controller should provide information about what they did in response to a request as soon as possible and in any case within one month of receiving the request.

- If it will take longer than one month, the controller must inform the person who made the request, within that month, and explain why it is taking so long.

- The controller should try to give the information in the same format it was received unless the person asks for something different. For example, if the request was received via email, the controller should respond via email.

- If the controller does not act on a request, they must inform the data subject within one month about why they did not take action. The data subject can complain to a supervisory authority and also seek judicial remedy.

- The information should be provided free of charge. However, if a data subject makes repetitive or excessive requests, the controller can charge a reasonable fee or refuse the request.

- If the controller has doubts about the identity of the person making the request, they can ask for more information to confirm their identity.

- The information that the controller must provide to data subjects about how they will use their data can be combined with standard icons. Standard icons can be used when explaining to people how the controller will process their personal data. This will help people understand what the controller is doing with their data in an easy way. If the icons are shown on a screen, they must be easy for machines to read too.

3

Article 13

Information to be Provided Where Personal Data is Collected From the Data Subject

Official GDPR Text

1. Where personal data relating to a data subject are collected from the data subject, the controller shall, at the time when personal data are obtained, provide the data subject with all of the following information:

   a. the identity and the contact details of the controller and, where applicable, of the controller's representative;

   b. the contact details of the data protection officer, where applicable;

   c. the purposes of the processing for which the personal data are intended as well as the legal basis for the processing;

   d. where the processing is based on point (f) of Article 6(1), the legitimate interests pursued by the controller or by a third party;

   e. the recipients or categories of recipients of the personal data, if any;

   f. where applicable, the fact that the controller intends to transfer personal data to a third country or international organisation and the existence or absence of an adequacy decision by the Commission, or in the case of transfers referred to in Article 46 or 47, or the second subparagraph of Article 49(1), reference to the appropriate or suitable safeguards and the means by which to obtain a copy of them or where they have been made available.

2. In addition to the information referred to in paragraph 1, the controller shall, at the time when personal data are obtained, provide the data subject with the following further information necessary to ensure fair and transparent processing:

   a. the period for which the personal data will be stored, or if that is not possible, the criteria used to determine that period;

   b. the existence of the right to request from the controller access to and rectification or erasure of personal data or restriction of processing concerning the data subject or to object to processing as well as the right to data portability;

   c. where the processing is based on point (a) of Article 6(1) or point (a) of Article 9(2), the existence of the right to withdraw consent at any time, without affecting the lawfulness of processing based on consent before its withdrawal;

   d. the right to lodge a complaint with a supervisory authority;

   e. whether the provision of personal data is a statutory or contractual requirement, or a requirement necessary to enter into a contract, as well as whether the data subject is obliged to provide the personal data and of the possible consequences of failure to provide such data;

   f. the existence of automated decision-making, including profiling, referred to in Article 22(1) and (4) and, at least in those cases, meaningful information about the logic involved, as well as the significance and the envisaged consequences of such processing for the data subject.

3

3. Where the controller intends to further process the personal data for a purpose other than that for which the personal data were collected, the controller shall provide the data subject prior to that further processing with information on that other purpose and with any relevant further information as referred to in paragraph 2.

4. Paragraphs 1, 2 and 3 shall not apply where and insofar as the data subject already has the information.

Easy Peasy Summary

*   Controllers should provide the data subject with the following information when collecting personal data:

    o   identity and contact details of the controller (and of the representative of the controller, if required);

    o   contact details of the data protection officer (DPO);

    o   reasons for the processing;

    o   legal basis for the processing;

    o   legitimate interest of the controller or a third party;

    o   details of any third party that will receive the personal data;

    o   details of any international transfers of personal data;

    o   how long they will keep personal data;

    o   whether their personal data is used for automated decision-making, including profiling;

○ rights available to the data subject:

- right to access, rectification and erasure of personal data;

- right to restrict;

- right to object;

- right to data portability;

- right to withdraw consent;

- right to file complaint with the supervisory authority.

○ Whether the data subject has to provide personal data because a law says so, such as employee salary details or for tax purposes;

○ Whether the data subject has to provide personal data because it is required to fulfil a contract, such as booking a hotel.

- If the controller wants to use personal data for a different purpose than what it was collected for, they must inform the data subject beforehand about the new purpose and provide the relevant information

- If the data subject already has this information, then it does not have to be provided

If the controller wants to use personal data for a different purpose ... they must inform the data subject ...

3

Article 14

Information to be Provided Where Personal Data Have Not Been Obtained from the Data Subject

Official GDPR Text

1. Where personal data have not been obtained from the data subject, the controller shall provide the data subject with the following information:

    a. the identity and the contact details of the controller and, where applicable, of the controller's representative;

    b. the contact details of the data protection officer, where applicable;

    c. the purposes of the processing for which the personal data are intended as well as the legal basis for the processing;

    d. the categories of personal data concerned;

    e. the recipients or categories of recipients of the personal data, if any;

    f. where applicable, that the controller intends to transfer personal data to a recipient in a third country or international organisation and the existence or absence of an adequacy decision by the Commission, or in the case of transfers referred to in Article 46 or 47, or the second subparagraph of Article 49(1), reference to the appropriate or suitable safeguards and the means to obtain a copy of them or where they have been made available.

2. In addition to the information referred to in paragraph 1, the controller shall provide the data subject with the following information necessary to ensure fair and transparent processing in respect of the data subject:

a. the period for which the personal data will be stored, or if that is not possible, the criteria used to determine that period;

b. where the processing is based on point (f) of Article 6(1), the legitimate interests pursued by the controller or by a third party;

c. the existence of the right to request from the controller access to and rectification or erasure of personal data or restriction of processing concerning the data subject and to object to processing as well as the right to data portability;

d. where processing is based on point (a) of Article 6(1) or point (a) of Article 9(2), the existence of the right to withdraw consent at any time, without affecting the lawfulness of processing based on consent before its withdrawal;

e. the right to lodge a complaint with a supervisory authority;

f. from which source the personal data originate, and if applicable, whether it came from publicly accessible sources;

g. the existence of automated decision-making, including profiling, referred to in Article 22(1) and (4) and, at least in those cases, meaningful information about the logic involved, as well as the significance and the envisaged consequences of such processing for the data subject.

3

3. The controller shall provide the information referred to in paragraphs 1 and 2:

   a. within a reasonable period after obtaining the personal data, but at the latest within one month, having regard to the specific circumstances in which the personal data are processed;

   b. if the personal data are to be used for communication with the data subject, at the latest at the time of the first communication to that data subject; or

   c. if a disclosure to another recipient is envisaged, at the latest when the personal data are first disclosed.

4. Where the controller intends to further process the personal data for a purpose other than that for which the personal data were obtained, the controller shall provide the data subject prior to that further processing with information on that other purpose and with any relevant further information as referred to in paragraph 2.

5. Paragraphs 1 to 4 shall not apply where and insofar as:

   a. the data subject already has the information;

   b. the provision of such information proves impossible or would involve a disproportionate effort, in particular for processing for archiving purposes in the public interest, scientific or historical research purposes or statistical purposes, subject to the conditions and safeguards referred to in Article 89(1) or in so far as the obligation referred to in paragraph 1 of this Article is likely to render impossible or seriously impair the achievement of the objectives of that processing. In such cases, the controller shall take appropriate measures to protect the data subject's rights and freedoms and legitimate interests, including making the information publicly available;

c.   obtaining or disclosure is expressly laid down by Union or Member State law to which the controller is subject and which provides appropriate measures to protect the data subject's legitimate interests; or

d.   where the personal data must remain confidential subject to an obligation of professional secrecy regulated by Union or Member State law, including a statutory obligation of secrecy.

3

Easy Peasy Summary

Where personal data is not collected directly from the data subject, controllers should provide the data subject with all the information mentioned in Article 13, and where they got the personal data from.

Article 15

Right of Access by the Data Subject

Official GDPR Text

1. The data subject shall have the right to obtain from the controller confirmation as to whether or not personal data concerning him or her are being processed, and, where that is the case, access to the personal data and the following information:

    a. the purposes of the processing;

    b. the categories of personal data concerned;

    c. the recipients or categories of recipient to whom the personal data have been or will be disclosed, in particular recipients in third countries or international organisations;

    d. where possible, the envisaged period for which the personal data will be stored, or, if not possible, the criteria used to determine that period;

    e. the existence of the right to request from the controller rectification or erasure of personal data or restriction of processing of personal data concerning the data subject or to object to such processing;

    f. the right to lodge a complaint with a supervisory authority;

    g. where the personal data are not collected from the data subject, any available information as to their source;

    h. the existence of automated decision-making, including profiling, referred to in Article 22(1) and (4) and, at least in those cases, meaningful information about the logic involved, as well as the significance and the envisaged consequences of such processing for the data subject.

2. Where personal data are transferred to a third country or to an international organisation, the data subject shall have the right to be informed of the appropriate safeguards pursuant to Article 46 relating to the transfer.

3. The controller shall provide a copy of the personal data undergoing processing. For any further copies requested by the data subject, the controller may charge a reasonable fee based on administrative costs. Where the data subject makes the request by electronic means, and unless otherwise requested by the data subject, the information shall be provided in a commonly used electronic form.

3

The right to obtain a copy … shall not adversely affect the rights and freedoms of others.

4. The right to obtain a copy referred to in paragraph 3 shall not adversely affect the rights and freedoms of others.

Easy Peasy Summary

- The data subject has the right to know:

  - whether their personal data is being processed;

  - what personal data is being processed;

  - the reasons for the processing;

  - the categories of personal data being processed;

  - how long the personal data will be kept;

  - third parties who will have access to their personal data;

  - the source from where the personal data is collected;

  - the existence of automated decision-making including profiling;

  - safety measures taken to secure the personal data in case of international transfers.

- The person has the right to ask the controller to correct or delete their personal data, limit the processing of their data, or object to how their data is being processed.

Information provided to the data subject should not include any information about other people.

- The data subject can complain to the supervisory authority.

- The controller should provide the data subject with a copy of their personal data that is being processed.

- Information provided to the data subject should not include any information about other people.

- The controller must give a copy of the data being processed.

- If the data subject wants more copies, the controller can charge a fee for administrative costs.

- If the request is made electronically, the information should be provided in a format that is widely used unless the data subject requests otherwise.

Article 16

Right to Rectification

Official GDPR Text

The data subject shall have the right to obtain from the controller without undue delay the rectification of inaccurate personal data concerning him or her. Taking into account the purposes of the processing, the data subject shall have the right to have incomplete personal data completed, including by means of providing a supplementary statement.

3

Easy Peasy Summary

The data subject has the right for any inaccurate or incomplete information about them to be corrected or updated immediately.

The data subject has the right for any inaccurate or incomplete information ... to be corrected ...

Article 17

Right to Erasure ('Right to be Forgotten')

Official GDPR Text

1. The data subject shall have the right to obtain from the controller the erasure of personal data concerning him or her without undue delay and the controller shall have the obligation to erase personal data without undue delay where one of the following grounds applies:

   a. the personal data are no longer necessary in relation to the purposes for which they were collected or otherwise processed;

   b. the data subject withdraws consent on which the processing is based according to point (a) of Article 6(1), or point (a) of Article 9(2), and where there is no other legal ground for the processing;

   c. the data subject objects to the processing pursuant to Article 21(1) and there are no overriding legitimate grounds for the processing, or the data subject objects to the processing pursuant to Article 21(2);

   d. the personal data have been unlawfully processed;

   e. the personal data have to be erased for compliance with a legal obligation in Union or Member State law to which the controller is subject;

   f. the personal data have been collected in relation to the offer of information society services referred to in Article 8(1).

2. Where the controller has made the personal data public and is obliged pursuant to paragraph 1 to erase the personal data, the controller, taking account of available technology and the cost of implementation, shall take reasonable steps, including technical measures, to inform controllers which are processing the personal data that the data subject has requested the erasure by such controllers of any links to, or copy or replication of, those personal data.

3

3. Paragraphs 1 and 2 shall not apply to the extent that processing is necessary:

   a. for exercising the right of freedom of expression and information;

   b. for compliance with a legal obligation which requires processing by Union or Member State law to which the controller is subject or for the performance of a task carried out in the public interest or in the exercise of official authority vested in the controller;

   c. for reasons of public interest in the area of public health in accordance with points (h) and (i) of Article 9(2) as well as Article 9(3);

   d. for archiving purposes in the public interest, scientific or historical research purposes or statistical purposes in accordance with Article 89(1) in so far as the right referred to in paragraph 1 is likely to render impossible or seriously impair the achievement of the objectives of that processing; or

   e. for the establishment, exercise or defence of legal claims.

Easy Peasy Summary

Data subjects have the right to request deletion of their personal data ...

- Data subjects have the right to request deletion of their personal data when:

    o personal data is no longer needed for the original purpose and no new lawful purpose exists;

    o the data subject withdraws their consent;

    o the data subject exercises the right to object (against the controller's legitimate interests) and the controller has no overriding grounds to continue processing;

    o the personal data has been processed unlawfully;

    o EU law or national law of the relevant Member State requires erasure.

- Where the personal data has been shared with other controllers, then it is the responsibility of the controller to inform the other controllers about the erasure request.

- The right to erasure is not available to be exercised when personal data is processed:

    o for exercising the right of freedom of expression and information;

    o to comply with a legal obligation;

    o for reasons of public interest in the area of public health;

    o for archiving for public interest reasons, scientific/ historical research purposes or statistical purposes; or

    o to establish, exercise or defend legal claims.

Article 18

Right to Restriction of Processing

Official GDPR Text

3

1. The data subject shall have the right to obtain from the controller restriction of processing where one of the following applies:

   a. the accuracy of the personal data is contested by the data subject, for a period enabling the controller to verify the accuracy of the personal data;

   b. the processing is unlawful and the data subject opposes the erasure of the personal data and requests the restriction of their use instead;

   c. the controller no longer needs the personal data for the purposes of the processing, but they are required by the data subject for the establishment, exercise or defence of legal claims;

   d. the data subject has objected to processing pursuant to Article 21(1) pending the verification whether the legitimate grounds of the controller override those of the data subject.

2. Where processing has been restricted under paragraph 1, such personal data shall, with the exception of storage, only be processed with the data subject's consent or for the establishment, exercise or defence of legal claims or for the protection of the rights of another natural or legal person or for reasons of important public interest of the Union or of a Member State.

3. A data subject who has obtained restriction of processing pursuant to paragraph 1 shall be informed by the controller before the restriction of processing is lifted.

Easy Peasy Summary

- The data subject can limit the controller from processing their personal data when:

  - the data subject disputes the accuracy of their data, the controller can take time to check and confirm its accuracy;

  - the data is being processed illegally but the data subject does not want it deleted;

  - the controller no longer needs the personal data for the purposes of the processing, but the data subject wants it in relation to a legal claim;

  - the data subject objects to the processing of their personal data and the controller is checking if they have any overriding grounds in relation to an erasure request or the controller's legitimate interests.

- Once the personal data is restricted, it can only be processed (with the exception of storage):

  - with the data subject's consent;

  - in relation to legal claims;

  - to protect the rights of another individual;

  - for the public interest.

Data subjects must be informed before the controller resumes processing.

- Data subjects must be informed before the controller resumes processing.

Article 19

Notification Obligation Regarding Rectification or Erasure of Personal Data or Restriction of Processing

Official GDPR Text

3

The controller shall communicate any rectification or erasure of personal data or restriction of processing carried out in accordance with Article 16, Article 17(1) and Article 18 to each recipient to whom the personal data have been disclosed, unless this proves impossible or involves disproportionate effort. The controller shall inform the data subject about those recipients if the data subject requests it.

Easy Peasy Summary

- The controller must inform third parties with whom they have shared the data subject's personal data, about the request for rectification, deletion and restriction.

- However, if this would be impossible or would take too much effort, the controller does not have to, such as when information was published in an article which was distributed at an event and there is no way of telling exactly who has a copy of the article.

- The controller needs to provide information about the third parties they shared the information with, if the data subject requests so.

The controller needs to provide information about the third parties they shared the information with...

Article 20
Right to Data Portability

Official GDPR Text

1. The data subject shall have the right to receive the personal data concerning him or her, which he or she has provided to a controller, in a structured, commonly used and machine-readable format and have the right to transmit those data to another controller without hindrance from the controller to which the personal data have been provided, where:

    a. the processing is based on consent pursuant to point (a) of Article 6(1) or point (a) of Article 9(2) or on a contract pursuant to point (b) of Article 6(1); and

    b. the processing is carried out by automated means.

2. In exercising his or her right to data portability pursuant to paragraph 1, the data subject shall have the right to have the personal data transmitted directly from one controller to another, where technically feasible.

3. The exercise of the right referred to in paragraph 1 of this Article shall be without prejudice to Article 17. That right shall not apply to processing necessary for the performance of a task carried out in the public interest or in the exercise of official authority vested in the controller.

4. The right referred to in paragraph 1 shall not adversely affect the rights and freedoms of others.

Easy Peasy Summary

- Data subjects have the right to ask for their personal data to be sent to another controller in a structured and common format that is readable by machines.

- Controllers must help the individual transfer the data to another organisation.

- This right to data portability is only applicable to personal data that is:

  o electronically processed; and

  o the personal data was collected directly from the data subject; and

  o if the processing is based on either consent or contractual necessity.

- Data portability rights do not apply when processing is required for the public interest or the exercise of official authority.

Data subjects have the right to ask for their personal data to be sent to another controller ...

3

Article 21
Right to Object

Official GDPR Text

1. The data subject shall have the right to object, on grounds relating to his or her particular situation, at any time to processing of personal data concerning him or her which is based on point (e) or (f) of Article 6(1), including profiling based on those provisions. The controller shall no longer process the personal data unless the controller demonstrates compelling legitimate grounds for the processing which override the interests, rights and freedoms of the data subject or for the establishment, exercise or defence of legal claims.

2. Where personal data are processed for direct marketing purposes, the data subject shall have the right to object at any time to processing of personal data concerning him or her for such marketing, which includes profiling to the extent that it is related to such direct marketing.

3. Where the data subject objects to processing for direct marketing purposes, the personal data shall no longer be processed for such purposes.

4. At the latest at the time of the first communication with the data subject, the right referred to in paragraphs 1 and 2 shall be explicitly brought to the attention of the data subject and shall be presented clearly and separately from any other information.

5. In the context of the use of information society services, and notwithstanding Directive 2002/58/EC, the data subject may exercise his or her right to object by automated means using technical specifications.

6. Where personal data are processed for scientific or historical research purposes or statistical purposes pursuant to Article 89(1), the data subject, on grounds relating to his or her particular situation, shall have the right to object to processing of personal data concerning him or her, unless the processing is necessary for the performance of a task carried out for reasons of public interest.

3

Easy Peasy Summary

•   This Article explains the conditions for when data subjects can object or request for the controller to stop processing their personal data.

•   The controller cannot process the personal data unless they have a strong reason that outweighs the data subject's rights and freedoms, or the processing is necessary for legal claims.

•   Data subjects can object to processing that is based on either public interests or legitimate interests.

•   The data subject has an absolute right to object to direct marketing or any profiling activities.

•   The rights mentioned in paragraphs 1 and 2 must be clearly and separately presented to the data subject when the controller first communicates with the data subject.

•   When a data subject objects to the processing of their personal data for scientific or historical research and for statistical purposes, the controller has to stop the processing, unless the controller can show that the processing is in the public interest.

The data subject has an absolute right to object to direct marketing or any profiling activities.

67

Article 22

Automated Individual Decision-making, Including Profiling

Official GDPR Text

1. The data subject shall have the right not to be subject to a decision based solely on automated processing, including profiling, which produces legal effects concerning him or her or similarly significantly affects him or her.

2. Paragraph 1 shall not apply if the decision:

    a. is necessary for entering into, or performance of, a contract between the data subject and a data controller;

    b. is authorised by Union or Member State law to which the controller is subject and which also lays down suitable measures to safeguard the data subject's rights and freedoms and legitimate interests; or

    c. is based on the data subject's explicit consent.

3. In the cases referred to in points (a) and (c) of paragraph 2, the data controller shall implement suitable measures to safeguard the data subject's rights and freedoms and legitimate interests, at least the right to obtain human intervention on the part of the controller, to express his or her point of view and to contest the decision.

4. Decisions referred to in paragraph 2 shall not be based on special categories of personal data referred to in Article 9(1), unless point (a) or (g) of Article 9(2) applies and suitable measures to safeguard the data subject's rights and freedoms and legitimate interests are in place.

Easy Peasy Summary

- This Article provides additional rules to protect personal data if the controller is solely relying on automated decision-making and if that decision-making will have legal effects or a significant impact on the individual.

- Data subjects have the right not to be subjected to automated individual decision-making, including profiling.

- The processing of personal data based solely on automated decision-making is allowed:

  - if it is important for entering into or the performance of a contract between the data subject and controller, such as a loan from the bank to check credit history; or

  - if the domestic or Union law applicable on the controller authorises them to do so; or

  - if the data subject has given explicit consent.

- The controller should take proper steps to protect the rights, freedom and the legitimate interests of data subjects.

- Decisions based on special categories of personal data can only be made if Article 9(2)(a) or (g) applies and measures are taken to protect the data subject's rights and interests.

The controller should take proper steps to protect the rights, freedom and legitimate interests of data subjects.

3

Article 23

Restrictions

Official GDPR Text

1. Union or Member State law to which the data controller or processor is subject may restrict by way of a legislative measure the scope of the obligations and rights provided for in Articles 12 to 22 and Article 34, as well as Article 5 in so far as its provisions correspond to the rights and obligations provided for in Articles 12 to 22, when such a restriction respects the essence of the fundamental rights and freedoms and is a necessary and proportionate measure in a democratic society to safeguard:

   a. national security;

   b. defence;

   c. public security;

   d. the prevention, investigation, detection or prosecution of criminal offences or the execution of criminal penalties, including the safeguarding against and the prevention of threats to public security;

   e. other important objectives of general public interest of the Union or of a Member State, in particular an important economic or financial interest of the Union or of a Member State, including monetary, budgetary and taxation matters, public health and social security;

   f. the protection of judicial independence and judicial proceedings;

   g. the prevention, investigation, detection and prosecution of breaches of ethics for regulated professions;

h. a monitoring, inspection or regulatory function connected, even occasionally, to the exercise of official authority in the cases referred to in points (a) to (e) and (g);

i. the protection of the data subject or the rights and freedoms of others;

j. the enforcement of civil law claims.

2. In particular, any legislative measure referred to in paragraph 1 shall contain specific provisions at least, where relevant, as to:

a. the purposes of the processing or categories of processing;

b. the categories of personal data;

c. the scope of the restrictions introduced;

d. the safeguards to prevent abuse or unlawful access or transfer;

e. the specification of the controller or categories of controllers;

f. the storage periods and the applicable safeguards taking into account the nature, scope and purposes of the processing or categories of processing;

g. the risks to the rights and freedoms of data subjects; and

h. the right of data subjects to be informed about the restriction, unless that may be prejudicial to the purpose of the restriction.

3

Easy Peasy Summary

- Member states can limit the rights of the data subject to safeguard:

  - national security;

  - defence;

  - public security;

  - the prevention, investigation, detection or prosecution of criminal offences or the execution of criminal penalties;

  - other important objectives of general public interest of the Union or of a Member State;

  - the protection of judicial independence and judicial proceedings;

  - the prevention, investigation, detection and prosecution of breaches of ethics for regulated professions;

  - monitoring, inspection or regulatory function connected, even occasionally, to the exercise of official authority;

  - the protection of the data subject or the rights and freedoms of others; or

  - the enforcement of civil law claims.

4

Controller and Processor

Article 24

Responsibility of the Controller

Official GDPR Text

1. Taking into account the nature, scope, context and purposes of processing, as well as the risks of varying likelihood and severity for the rights and freedoms of natural persons, the controller shall implement appropriate technical and organisational measures to ensure and to be able to demonstrate that processing is performed in accordance with this Regulation. Those measures shall be reviewed and updated where necessary.

2. Where proportionate in relation to processing activities, the measures referred to in paragraph 1 shall include the implementation of appropriate data protection policies by the controller.

3. Adherence to approved codes of conduct as referred to in Article 40 or approved certification mechanisms as referred to in Article 42 may be used as an element by which to demonstrate compliance with the obligations of the controller.

Easy Peasy Summary

*   Controllers must put in place sufficient technological and organisational/administrative processes. When they do so, they must consider:

    o   the type and extent of processing activities;

    o   the purpose of their processing activities;

- o the possibility and seriousness of the risks posed to the rights and freedom of data subjects by their processing activities;

- o the appropriateness of measures put in place.

- Such measures may include:

  - o implementing internal data protection policies;

  - o complying with codes of conduct recognised by the European Data Protection Board; and

  - o obtaining certifications recognised by the European Data Protection Board.

Article 25

Data Protection by Design and Default

Official GDPR Text

1. Taking into account the state-of-the-art, the cost of implementation and the nature, scope, context and purposes of processing as well as the risks of varying likelihood and severity for rights and freedoms of natural persons posed by the processing, the controller shall, both at the time of the determination of the means for processing and at the time of the processing itself, implement appropriate technical and organisational measures, such as pseudonymisation, which are designed to implement data-protection principles, such as data minimisation, in an effective manner and to integrate the necessary safeguards into the processing in order to meet the requirements of this Regulation and protect the rights of data subjects.

2. The controller shall implement appropriate technical and organisational measures for ensuring that, by default, only personal data which are necessary for each specific purpose of the processing are processed. That obligation applies to the amount of personal data collected, the extent of their processing, the period of their storage and their accessibility. In particular, such measures shall ensure that by default personal data are not made accessible without the individual's intervention to an indefinite number of natural persons.

3. An approved certification mechanism pursuant to Article 42 may be used as an element to demonstrate compliance with the requirements set out in paragraphs 1 and 2 of this Article.

4

Easy Peasy Summary

- Controllers should implement technical and organisational systems that are designed to:

  o comply with data protection principles;

  o respect the data subject's rights; and

  o guarantee the requirements of safe and secure processing.

- In doing so, they must consider:

  o what solutions are widely used by industry peers and experts;

  o the cost of implementing those systems;

  o the type and extent of processing activities;

  o the reasons for their processing activities; and

  o the possibility and seriousness of the risks posed to the rights and freedom of data subjects from processing activities.

... only personal data required for each specific purpose is collected ...

- Controllers should ensure that by default:

  o only personal data required for each specific purpose is collected;

  o processing is limited to only what is required to achieve the specific purpose;

  o personal data is stored only for the period required to meet the purpose it was collected for;

  o personal data is accessible to a limited number of people and that it is made available only to those who need to access it for the reasons for which it was collected.

Article 26

Joint Controllers

Official GDPR Text

1. Where two or more controllers jointly determine the purposes and means of processing, they shall be joint controllers. They shall in a transparent manner determine their respective responsibilities for compliance with the obligations under this Regulation, in particular as regards the exercising of the rights of the data subject and their respective duties to provide the information referred to in Articles 13 and 14, by means of an arrangement between them unless, and in so far as, the respective responsibilities of the controllers are determined by Union or Member State law to which the controllers are subject. The arrangement may designate a contact point for data subjects.

2. The arrangement referred to in paragraph 1 shall duly reflect the respective roles and relationships of the joint controllers vis-à-vis the data subjects. The essence of the arrangement shall be made available to the data subject.

3. Irrespective of the terms of the arrangement referred to in paragraph 1, the data subject may exercise his or her rights under this Regulation in respect of and against each of the controllers.

4

Easy Peasy Summary

Joint controllers must share controller obligations.

- Joint controllers decide together why and how personal data is processed.

- Joint controllers must share controller obligations.

- The division of their obligations must be clear and made public (unless the distribution of responsibilities is based on national law or EU law).

- The division of responsibilities must reflect the nature of the relationship between each controller and the data subjects.

- It is acceptable for a contact point to be assigned for data subjects to direct their queries to.

- Regardless of how these obligations are shared, data subjects can exercise their rights against either controller.

Article 27

Representatives of Controllers or Processors Not Established in the Union

Official GDPR Text

1. Where Article 3(2) applies, the controller or the processor shall designate in writing a representative in the Union.

2. The obligation laid down in paragraph 1 of this Article shall not apply to:

   a. processing which is occasional, does not include, on a large scale, processing of special categories of data as referred to in Article 9(1) or processing of personal data relating to criminal convictions and offences referred to in Article 10, and is unlikely to result in a risk to the rights and freedoms of natural persons, taking into account the nature, context, scope and purposes of the processing; or

   b. a public authority or body.

3. The representative shall be established in one of the Member States where the data subjects, whose personal data are processed in relation to the offering of goods or services to them, or whose behaviour is monitored, are.

4. The representative shall be mandated by the controller or processor to be addressed in addition to or instead of the controller or the processor by, in particular, supervisory authorities and data subjects, on all issues related to processing, for the purposes of ensuring compliance with this Regulation.

5. The designation of a representative by the controller or processor shall be without prejudice to legal actions which could be initiated against the controller or the processor themselves.

Easy Peasy Summary

The appointment of the representative must be in writing.

- Controllers and processors who fall within the scope of the Regulation but are not established in the European Union, must appoint a representative within the European Union.

- The appointment of the representative must be in writing.

- The representative should be located in the Member state of the data subjects they are doing business with, or are monitoring.

- Appointing a representative will not affect the ability to bring legal action directly against the controllers or processors represented.

- The following are exempt from this requirement:

  o those who process personal data occasionally and where that processing does not involve processing special categories of data on a large scale; and

  o public authorities.

Article 28

Processor

Official GDPR Text

1. Where processing is to be carried out on behalf of a controller, the controller shall use only processors providing sufficient guarantees to implement appropriate technical and organisational measures in such a manner that processing will meet the requirements of this Regulation and ensure the protection of the rights of the data subject.

2. The processor shall not engage another processor without prior specific or general written authorisation of the controller. In the case of general written authorisation, the processor shall inform the controller of any intended changes concerning the addition or replacement of other processors, thereby giving the controller the opportunity to object to such changes.

3. Processing by a processor shall be governed by a contract or other legal act under Union or Member State law, that is binding on the processor with regard to the controller and that sets out the subject-matter and duration of the processing, the nature and purpose of the processing, the type of personal data and categories of data subjects and the obligations and rights of the controller. That contract or other legal act shall stipulate, in particular, that the processor:

   a. processes the personal data only on documented instructions from the controller, including with regard to transfers of personal data to a third country or an international organisation, unless required to do so by Union or Member State law to which the processor is subject; in such a case, the processor shall inform the controller of that legal requirement before processing, unless that law prohibits such information on important grounds of public interest;

4

b. ensures that persons authorised to process the personal data have committed themselves to confidentiality or are under an appropriate statutory obligation of confidentiality;

c. takes all measures required pursuant to Article 32;

d. respects the conditions referred to in paragraphs 2 and 4 for engaging another processor;

e. taking into account the nature of the processing, assists the controller by appropriate technical and organisational measures, insofar as this is possible, for the fulfilment of the controller's obligation to respond to requests for exercising the data subject's rights laid down in Chapter III;

f. assists the controller in ensuring compliance with the obligations pursuant to Articles 32 to 36 taking into account the nature of processing and the information available to the processor;

g. at the choice of the controller, deletes or returns all the personal data to the controller after the end of the provision of services relating to processing, and deletes existing copies unless Union or Member State law requires storage of the personal data;

h. makes available to the controller all information necessary to demonstrate compliance with the obligations laid down in this Article and allow for and contribute to audits, including inspections, conducted by the controller or another auditor mandated by the controller.

4. With regard to point (h) of the first subparagraph, the processor shall immediately inform the controller if, in its opinion, an instruction infringes this Regulation or other Union or Member State data protection provisions.

5. Where a processor engages another processor for carrying out specific processing activities on behalf of the controller, the same data protection obligations as set out in the contract or other legal act between the controller and the processor as referred to in paragraph 3 shall be imposed on that other processor by way of a contract or other legal act under Union or Member State law, in particular providing sufficient guarantees to implement appropriate technical and organisational measures in such a manner that the processing will meet the requirements of this Regulation. Where that other processor fails to fulfil its data protection obligations, the initial processor shall remain fully liable to the controller for the performance of that other processor's obligations.

4

6. Adherence of a processor to an approved code of conduct as referred to in Article 40 or an approved certification mechanism as referred to in Article 42 may be used as an element by which to demonstrate sufficient guarantees as referred to in paragraphs 1 and 4 of this Article.

7. Without prejudice to an individual contract between the controller and the processor, the contract or the other legal act referred to in paragraphs 3 and 4 of this Article may be based, in whole or in part, on standard contractual clauses referred to in paragraphs 7 and 8 of this Article, including when they are part of a certification granted to the controller or processor pursuant to Articles 42 and 43.

8. The Commission may lay down standard contractual clauses for the matters referred to in paragraph 3 and 4 of this Article and in accordance with the examination procedure referred to in Article 93(2).

9. A supervisory authority may adopt standard contractual clauses for the matters referred to in paragraph 3 and 4 of this Article and in accordance with the consistency mechanism referred to in Article 63.

10. The contract or the other legal act referred to in paragraphs 3 and 4 shall be in writing, including in electronic form.

11. Without prejudice to Articles 82, 83 and 84, if a processor infringes this Regulation by determining the purposes and means of processing, the processor shall be considered to be a controller in respect of that processing.

Easy Peasy Summary

- Controllers may only use processors that can demonstrate that they will put in place the required technical and organisational measures to make sure the personal data is kept protected and private and can fulfil the obligations of this Regulation.

- Processors must not appoint sub-processors to process personal data without the prior written authorisation of the controller.

- The relationship between the controller and processor must be set out in a contract between the parties or a binding legal act under national law or European Union laws.

- The contract or legal act must explain:

  o the nature and purpose of processing;

  o what categories of personal data will be processed;

  o how long the processing will go on for;

  o the categories of data subjects;

  o the rights and responsibilities of the controller;

o that the processor can only process data or transfer data to third countries and international organisations on the documented instructions of the controller or where required to do so by national law or European Union law. Where required to do so by national law or European Union law, the processor must inform the controller of such a law before processing (except where the law prevents doing so on the grounds of public interest);

o that individuals who are authorised by the processor to process the data must be under a confidentiality obligation;

o that they will take all measures to ensure an appropriate level of security to tackle the risks posed to the personal data by its processing activities;

o that the processor will consent from controller before engaging any sub-processor, and will ensure written commitments are in place with the sub-processors which are no less onerous than the present contract/legal act;

o that the processor guarantees to assist the controller to fulfil their obligations under the Regulation by putting in place appropriate technical and organisation measures;

o that the processor must assist the controller to comply with its obligations;

o that, depending on the preference of the controller, the processor must delete or return all personal data at the end of the service.

- If the processor thinks that an instruction violates this regulation or other data protection rules, they must tell the controller right away.

... individuals who are authorised by the processor to process the data must be under a confidentiality obligation ...

4

- Processors must ensure that sub-processors are under the same obligations imposed on the processor by the controller (either by contract or a legal act under national law or European law).

- The processor will be fully liable to the controller where sub-processors violate the processor's obligations.

- The contractual agreement or legal act between the controller-processor and/or processor-sub-processor relationship must be in writing, even when it is in an electronic format.

- A processor that decides how and why processing is carried out will be considered a controller.

Article 29

Processing Under the Authority of the Controller or Processor

Official GDPR Text

The processor and any person acting under the authority of the controller or of the processor, who has access to personal data, shall not process those data except on instructions from the controller, unless required to do so by Union or Member State law.

4

Easy Peasy Summary

Processors can only process personal data as instructed in writing by the controller.

... only process personal data as instructed in writing by the controller.

Article 30

Records of Processing Activities

Official GDPR Text

1. Each controller and, where applicable, the controller's representative, shall maintain a record of processing activities under its responsibility. That record shall contain all of the following information:

   a. the name and contact details of the controller and, where applicable, the joint controller, the controller's representative and the data protection officer;

   b. the purposes of the processing;

   c. a description of the categories of data subjects and of the categories of personal data;

   d. the categories of recipients to whom the personal data have been or will be disclosed including recipients in third countries or international organisations;

   e. where applicable, transfers of personal data to a third country or an international organisation, including the identification of that third country or international organisation and, in the case of transfers referred to in the second subparagraph of Article 49(1), the documentation of suitable safeguards;

   f. where possible, the envisaged time limits for erasure of the different categories of data;

   g. where possible, a general description of the technical and organisational security measures referred to in Article 32(1).

2. Each processor and, where applicable, the processor's representative, shall maintain a record of all categories of processing activities carried out on behalf of a controller, containing:

   a. the name and contact details of the processor or processors and of each controller on behalf of which the processor is acting and, where applicable, of the controller's or the processor's representative, and the data protection officer;

   b. the categories of processing carried out on behalf of each controller;

   c. where applicable, transfers of personal data to a third country or an international organisation, including the identification of that third country or international organisation and, in the case of transfers referred to in the second subparagraph of Article 49(1), the documentation of suitable safeguards;

   d. where possible, a general description of the technical and organisational security measures referred to in Article 32(1).

3. The records referred to in paragraphs 1 and 2 shall be in writing, including in electronic form.

4. The controller or the processor and, where applicable, the controller's or the processor's representative, shall make the record available to the supervisory authority on request.

5. The obligations referred to in paragraphs 1 and 2 shall not apply to an enterprise or an organisation employing fewer than 250 persons,

   a. unless the processing it carries out is likely to result in a risk to the rights and freedoms of data subjects,

4

b. the processing is not occasional, or the processing includes special categories of data as referred to in Article 9(1) or personal data relating to criminal convictions and offences referred to in Article 10.

Easy Peasy Summary

Controllers should keep a record of all their processing activities.

- Controllers should keep a record of all their processing activities.

- The records should include:

  o the name and contact details of:

    - the controller and/or joint controller, if applicable;

    - the European Union representative; and

    - the data protection officer;

  o the purpose of processing;

  o the categories of data subject;

  o the categories of personal data;

  o the categories of third parties that personal data will be shared or disclosed to (including those in third countries);

  o the details of any third country transfers;

  o the storage period of the personal data;

  o a general description of the organisational and technical measures to keep the data secure and private.

- Processors should also keep a record of the processing activities it carries out on behalf of each controller.

- The records must be in writing and there should be an electronic copy.

- The records must be made available to the supervisory authority upon request.

- Keeping records of processing activity is mandatory when:

  ○ an organisation has 250 employees or more; or

  ○ processing is likely to result in a risk to rights and freedoms of the data subject; or

  ○ processing is not a one-off; or

  ○ processing includes special categories of data or data about criminal convictions or offences.

The records must be made available to the supervisory authority upon request.

4

Article 31

Cooperation With the Supervisory Authority

Official GDPR Text

The controller and the processor and, where applicable, their representatives, shall cooperate, on request, with the supervisory authority in the performance of its tasks.

Easy Peasy Summary

Controllers, processors and their representatives must cooperate with supervisory authorities.

Article 32
Security of Processing

Official GDPR Text

1. Taking into account the state-of-the-art, the costs of implementation and the nature, scope, context and purposes of processing, as well as the risk of varying likelihood and severity for the rights and freedoms of natural persons, the controller and the processor shall implement appropriate technical and organisational measures to ensure a level of security appropriate to the risk, including inter alia as appropriate:

   a. the pseudonymisation and encryption of personal data;

   b. the ability to ensure the ongoing confidentiality, integrity, availability and resilience of processing systems and services;

   c. the ability to restore the availability and access to personal data in a timely manner in the event of a physical or technical incident;

   d. a process for regularly testing, assessing and evaluating the effectiveness of technical and organisational measures for ensuring the security of the processing.

2. In assessing the appropriate level of security account shall be taken in particular of the risks that are presented by processing, in particular from accidental or unlawful destruction, loss, alteration, unauthorised disclosure of, or access to personal data transmitted, stored or otherwise processed.

4

3. Adherence to an approved code of conduct as referred to in Article 40 or an approved certification mechanism as referred to in Article 42 may be used as an element by which to demonstrate compliance with the requirements set out in paragraph 1 of this Article.

4. The controller and processor shall take steps to ensure that any natural person acting under the authority of the controller or the processor who has access to personal data does not process them except on instructions from the controller, unless he or she is required to do so by Union or Member State law.

Easy Peasy Summary

- Controllers and processors must put in place technical and organisational systems that are designed to make sure an appropriate level of security is in place to mitigate the risks of processing.

- Controllers and processors should think about the following when implementing appropriate technical and organisational solutions:

  o state-of-the-art technology;

  o the cost of implementing those systems;

  o the type and extent of processing activities;

  o the reasons for their processing activities;

  o the possibility and seriousness of the risks posed to the rights and freedom of data subjects as a result of the processing;

  o the nature of the risks because of the processing activities.

- Compliance with an approved code of conduct or certification mechanism can be used to demonstrate the controller has met their security obligations.

- Controllers and processors must make sure that systems are in place so that anyone acting under their instructions, such as an employee or contractor, does not process personal data other than when they have been asked to do so (or when required by national or European Union law).

Controllers and processors must make sure that systems are in place ...

4

Article 33

Notification of a Personal Data Breach to the Supervisory Authority

Official GDPR Text

1. In the case of a personal data breach, the controller shall without undue delay and, where feasible, not later than 72 hours after having become aware of it, notify the personal data breach to the supervisory authority competent in accordance with Article 55, unless the personal data breach is unlikely to result in a risk to the rights and freedoms of natural persons. Where the notification to the supervisory authority is not made within 72 hours, it shall be accompanied by reasons for the delay.

2. The processor shall notify the controller without undue delay after becoming aware of a personal data breach.

3. The notification referred to in paragraph 1 shall at least:

   a. describe the nature of the personal data breach including, where possible, the categories and approximate number of data subjects concerned and the categories and approximate number of personal data records concerned;

   b. communicate the name and contact details of the data protection officer or other contact point where more information can be obtained;

   c. describe the likely consequences of the personal data breach;

   d. describe the measures taken or proposed to be taken by the controller to address the personal data breach, including, where appropriate, measures to mitigate its possible adverse effects.

4. Where, and in so far as, it is not possible to provide the information at the same time, the information may be provided in phases without undue further delay.

5. The controller shall document any personal data breaches, comprising the facts relating to the personal data breach, its effects and the remedial action taken. That documentation shall enable the supervisory authority to verify compliance with this Article.

Easy Peasy Summary

Processors must inform controllers about any personal data breaches as soon as possible.

4

- Processors must inform controllers about any personal data breaches as soon as possible.

- Processors must put in place measures to detect incidents.

- If a breach is likely to pose a risk to the rights and freedom of the data subject, the controller must report it to the concerned supervisory authority.

- The report must be made:

  o as soon as possible; or

  o within 72 hours after the controller knows of the breach.

- If a data breach is reported after 72 hours, the controller must give reasons for the delay.

- The report must include:

  o the nature of the breach including:

  • the categories of data subjects;

  • how many data subjects are affected; and

  • the number of personal data records affected.

- ○ the name and contact details of the data protection officer;

- ○ the possible impacts on the data subject because of the breach;

- ○ what has been done or will be done to address and/or mitigate the breach.

Controllers must keep records of all personal data breaches ...

- Controllers must keep records of all personal data breaches, including the facts of the breach, its effects and remedial actions so supervisory authorities can assess compliance with the Regulation.

Article 34

Communication of Personal Data Breach to the Data Subject

Official GDPR Text

1. When the personal data breach is likely to result in a high risk to the rights and freedoms of natural persons, the controller shall communicate the personal data breach to the data subject without undue delay.

2. The communication to the data subject referred to in paragraph 1 of this Article shall describe in clear and plain language the nature of the personal data breach and contain at least the information and measures referred to in points (b), (c) and (d) of Article 33(3).

3. The communication to the data subject referred to in paragraph 1 shall not be required if any of the following conditions are met:

   a. the controller has implemented appropriate technical and organisational protection measures, and those measures were applied to the personal data affected by the personal data breach, in particular those that render the personal data unintelligible to any person who is not authorised to access it, such as encryption;

   b. the controller has taken subsequent measures which ensure that the high risk to the rights and freedoms of data subjects referred to in paragraph 1 is no longer likely to materialise;

   c. it would involve disproportionate effort. In such a case, there shall instead be a public communication or similar measure whereby the data subjects are informed in an equally effective manner.

4

4. If the controller has not already communicated the personal data breach to the data subject, the supervisory authority, having considered the likelihood of the personal data breach resulting in a high risk, may require it to do so or may decide that any of the conditions referred to in paragraph 3 are met.

Easy Peasy Summary

- When a personal data breach is likely to present high risks to the rights and freedoms of individuals, the controller must tell the data subjects about the breach.

The data subjects should be informed as soon as possible.

- The data subjects should be informed as soon as possible.

- The communication should be written in clear and plain language.

- The information that must be provided to the data subject includes:

  o the nature of the breach;

  o the name and contact details of the data protection officer;

  o the possible impacts of the breach; and

  o what has been done or will be done to address the breach.

- The controller does not need to let the data subjects know if:

  o there was no impact on the personal data because of prior measures that were in place; or

  o actions taken by the controller after the breach have greatly reduced the risk; or

○ providing individual notice to the data subjects would require too much effort. Where that is the case, the controller must make a public announcement, for example, a press release or statement on a website.

4

Article 35

Data Protection Impact Assessment

Official GDPR Text

1. Where a type of processing in particular using new technologies, and taking into account the nature, scope, context and purposes of the processing, is likely to result in a high risk to the rights and freedoms of natural persons, the controller shall, prior to the processing, carry out an assessment of the impact of the envisaged processing operations on the protection of personal data. A single assessment may address a set of similar processing operations that present similar high risks.

2. The controller shall seek the advice of the data protection officer, where designated, when carrying out a data protection impact assessment.

3. A data protection impact assessment referred to in paragraph 1 shall in particular be required in the case of:

    a. a systematic and extensive evaluation of personal aspects relating to natural persons which is based on automated processing, including profiling, and on which decisions are based that produce legal effects concerning the natural person or similarly significantly affect the natural person;

    b. processing on a large scale of special categories of data referred to in Article 9(1), or of personal data relating to criminal convictions and offences referred to in Article 10; or

    c. a systematic monitoring of a publicly accessible area on a large scale.

4. The supervisory authority shall establish and make public a list of the kind of processing operations which are subject to the requirement for a data protection impact assessment pursuant to paragraph 1. The supervisory authority shall communicate those lists to the Board referred to in Article 68.

5. The supervisory authority may also establish and make public a list of the kind of processing operations for which no data protection impact assessment is required. The supervisory authority shall communicate those lists to the Board.

6. Prior to the adoption of the lists referred to in paragraphs 4 and 5, the competent supervisory authority shall apply the consistency mechanism referred to in Article 63 where such lists involve processing activities which are related to the offering of goods or services to data subjects or to the monitoring of their behaviour in several Member States, or may substantially affect the free movement of personal data within the Union.

7. The assessment shall contain at least:

   a. a systematic description of the envisaged processing operations and the purposes of the processing, including, where applicable, the legitimate interest pursued by the controller;

   b. an assessment of the necessity and proportionality of the processing operations in relation to the purposes;

   c. an assessment of the risks to the rights and freedoms of data subjects referred to in paragraph 1; and

   d. the measures envisaged to address the risks, including safeguards, security measures and mechanisms to ensure the protection of personal data and to demonstrate compliance with this Regulation taking into account the rights and legitimate interests of data subjects and other persons concerned.

4

8. Compliance with approved codes of conduct referred to in Article 40 by the relevant controllers or processors shall be taken into due account in assessing the impact of the processing operations performed by such controllers or processors, in particular for the purposes of a data protection impact assessment.

9. Where appropriate, the controller shall seek the views of data subjects or their representatives on the intended processing, without prejudice to the protection of commercial or public interests or the security of processing operations.

10. Where processing pursuant to point (c) or (e) of Article 6(1) has a legal basis in Union law or in the law of the Member State to which the controller is subject, that law regulates the specific processing operation or set of operations in question, and a data protection impact assessment has already been carried out as part of a general impact assessment in the context of the adoption of that legal basis, paragraphs 1 to 7 shall not apply unless Member States deem it to be necessary to carry out such an assessment prior to processing activities.

11. Where necessary, the controller shall carry out a review to assess if processing is performed in accordance with the data protection impact assessment at least when there is a change of the risk represented by processing operations.

Easy Peasy Summary

- If the planned processing activity is going to create high risks to the rights and freedoms of data subjects, the controller must carry out an impact assessment called the Data Protection Impact Assessment (DPIA).

- When assessing the risks, the controller must think about:

  o the nature and scope of the processing activity;

  o the context in which the processing will take place; and

  o the reasons for the processing.

- Some instances where a Data Protection Impact Assessment could be required include:

  o when using new technologies;

  o when processing involves automated decision-making, including profiling;

  o when processing special category data and data about criminal convictions and offences on a large scale; and

  o when public areas are monitored systematically on a large scale.

- A data protection officer must be involved when carrying out a DPIA.

- Supervisory authorities must publish a list of processing operations that require a DPIA.

- A DPIA should include:

  o a detailed description of the planned processing activity;

  o the reason for the processing;

  o the legal basis for the processing;

A data protection officer must be involved when carrying out a DPIA.

4

- o how necessary and appropriate the processing activity is to meet the reason for the processing;

- o the potential risks to the rights and freedoms of data subjects; and

- o what the controller will do to address and reduce or remove the potential risks identified.

- Controllers should speak with the data subjects or their representatives about the planned processing activity and take into account what they think.

- The controller must review whether the processing aligns with the data protection impact assessment, especially if there is a change in the risk associated with processing.

Article 36

Prior Consultation

Official GDPR Text

1. The controller shall consult the supervisory authority prior to processing where a data protection impact assessment under Article 35 indicates that the processing would result in a high risk in the absence of measures taken by the controller to mitigate the risk.

4

2. Where the supervisory authority is of the opinion that the intended processing referred to in paragraph 1 would infringe this Regulation, in particular where the controller has insufficiently identified or mitigated the risk, the supervisory authority shall, within period of up to eight weeks of receipt of the request for consultation, provide written advice to the controller and, where applicable to the processor, and may use any of its powers referred to in Article 58. That period may be extended by six weeks, taking into account the complexity of the intended processing. The supervisory authority shall inform the controller and, where applicable, the processor, of any such extension within one month of receipt of the request for consultation together with the reasons for the delay. Those periods may be suspended until the supervisory authority has obtained information it has requested for the purposes of the consultation.

3. When consulting the supervisory authority pursuant to paragraph 1, the controller shall provide the supervisory authority with:

   a. where applicable, the respective responsibilities of the controller, joint controllers and processors involved in the processing, in particular for processing within a group of undertakings;

b. the purposes and means of the intended processing;

c. the measures and safeguards provided to protect the rights and freedoms of data subjects pursuant to this Regulation;

d. where applicable, the contact details of the data protection officer;

e. the data protection impact assessment provided for in Article 35; and

f. any other information requested by the supervisory authority.

4. Member States shall consult the supervisory authority during the preparation of a proposal for a legislative measure to be adopted by a national parliament, or of a regulatory measure based on such a legislative measure, which relates to processing.

5. Notwithstanding paragraph 1, Member State law may require controllers to consult with, and obtain prior authorisation from, the supervisory authority in relation to processing by a controller for the performance of a task carried out by the controller in the public interest, including processing in relation to social protection and public health.

Easy Peasy Summary

- When a Data Protection Impact Assessment shows the planned processing will create a high risk and that high risk cannot be reduced or removed, the controller must consult the supervisory authority.

- The supervisory authority should offer advice within 8 weeks of receiving the request. They can take up to another 6 weeks if it is particularly complicated or difficult.

- The supervisory authority must notify the controller and, if relevant, the processor, about any extension within one month of receiving the consultation request, along with the reasons for the delay.

- The timeframes can be paused until the authority receives the necessary information for the consultation.

... timeframes can be paused until the authority receives the necessary information ...

- When consulting with the supervisory authority, the controller needs to share:

  o The roles and responsibilities of all parties involved in the data processing, especially within a group of companies.

  o The goals and methods of the planned data processing.

  o Steps taken to safeguard the rights and freedoms of individuals, as per the rules.

  o The contact details of the data protection officer, if applicable.

  o The data protection impact assessment, as required by Article 35.

  o Any additional information the supervisory authority asks for.

- When creating a data processing-related law or regulation, Member States need to consult with the supervisory authority.

- Regardless of paragraph 1, a Member State's law may ask controllers to consult and get approval from the supervisory authority for data processing related to public interest tasks, including social protection and public health.

4

Article 37

Designation of the Data Protection Officer

Official GDPR Text

1. The controller and the processor shall designate a data protection officer in any case where:

    a. the processing is carried out by a public authority or body, except for courts acting in their judicial capacity;

    b. the core activities of the controller or the processor consist of processing operations which, by virtue of their nature, their scope and/or their purposes, require regular and systematic monitoring of data subjects on a large scale; or

    c. the core activities of the controller or the processor consist of processing on a large scale of special categories of data pursuant to Article 9 and personal data relating to criminal convictions and offences referred to in Article 10.

2. A group of undertakings may appoint a single data protection officer provided that a data protection officer is easily accessible from each establishment.

3. Where the controller or the processor is a public authority or body, a single data protection officer may be designated for several such authorities or bodies, taking account of their organisational structure and size.

4. In cases other than those referred to in paragraph 1, the controller or processor or associations and other bodies representing categories of controllers or processors may or, where required by Union or Member State law shall, designate a data protection officer. The data protection officer may act for such associations and other bodies representing controllers or processors.

5. The data protection officer shall be designated on the basis of professional qualities and, in particular, expert knowledge of data protection law and practices and the ability to fulfil the tasks referred to in Article 39.

6. The data protection officer may be a staff member of the controller or processor, or fulfil the tasks on the basis of a service contract.

7. The controller or the processor shall publish the contact details of the data protection officer and communicate them to the supervisory authority.

4

Easy Peasy Summary

•   The controller and processor must appoint a data protection officer when:

    ○   processing is carried out by a public authority;

    ○   the main business activities of the controller or processor include regular and systematic monitoring of individuals on large scale; or

    ○   the main business activities include processing of special categories of personal data on a large scale.

•   A group of companies can appoint a single data protection officer. The DPO should be easily reachable by all group members/subsidiaries.

•   The data protection officer can be an employee of the controller or processor, or a consultancy such as Kazient Privacy Experts, and work based on a service agreement.

- The controller or processor must share the data protection officer's contact information publicly and provide it to the supervisory authority.

- The DPO must:

  o have expert working knowledge of data protection law; and

  o have the ability to fulfil the tasks listed in Article 39.

Article 38

Position of the Data Protection Officer

Official GDPR Text

1. The controller and the processor shall ensure that the data protection officer is involved, properly and in a timely manner, in all issues which relate to the protection of personal data.

2. The controller and processor shall support the data protection officer in performing the tasks referred to in Article 39 by providing resources necessary to carry out those tasks and access to personal data and processing operations, and to maintain his or her expert knowledge.

3. The controller and processor shall ensure that the data protection officer does not receive any instructions regarding the exercise of those tasks. He or she shall not be dismissed or penalised by the controller or the processor for performing his tasks. The data protection officer shall directly report to the highest management level of the controller or the processor.

4. Data subjects may contact the data protection officer with regard to all issues related to processing of their personal data and to the exercise of their rights under this Regulation.

5. The data protection officer shall be bound by secrecy or confidentiality concerning the performance of his or her tasks, in accordance with Union or Member State law.

6. The data protection officer may fulfil other tasks and duties. The controller or processor shall ensure that any such tasks and duties do not result in a conflict of interests.

4

Easy Peasy Summary

The controller and processor must make sure that the DPO:

- is involved in all matters related to protecting of personal data sufficiently early;

- is empowered to perform their tasks and provided with the resources necessary;

- is not interfered with or punished for performing their tasks;

- reports to the most senior level of management of the controller or processor;

- can be contacted by data subjects about the processing of their data and their data subject rights;

- is bound by confidentiality; and

- does not have another role that will create conflict with their DPO duties.

Article 39

Tasks of the Data Protection Officer

Official GDPR Text

1. The data protection officer shall have at least the following tasks:

    a. to inform and advise the controller or the processor and the employees who carry out processing of their obligations pursuant to this Regulation and to other Union or Member State data protection provisions;

    b. to monitor compliance with this Regulation, with other Union or Member State data protection provisions and with the policies of the controller or processor in relation to the protection of personal data, including the assignment of responsibilities, awareness-raising and training of staff involved in processing operations, and the related audits;

    c. to provide advice where requested as regards the data protection impact assessment and monitor its performance pursuant to Article 35;

    d. to cooperate with the supervisory authority;

    e. to act as the contact point for the supervisory authority on issues relating to processing, including the prior consultation referred to in Article 36, and to consult, where appropriate, with regard to any other matter.

2. The data protection officer shall in the performance of his or her tasks have due regard to the risk associated with processing operations, taking into account the nature, scope, context and purposes of processing.

4

Easy Peasy Summary

The DPO has a duty to:

- inform and advise controllers, processors and their employees of what they are required to do;

- monitor whether the organisation is complying with data protection laws;

- provide advice on data protection issues;

- cooperate with the supervisory authority;

- act as the contact point for the supervisory authority; and

- conduct audits.

Article 40

Codes of Conduct

Official GDPR Text

1. The Member States, the supervisory authority, the Board and the Commission shall encourage the drawing up of codes of conduct intended to contribute to the proper application of this Regulation, taking account of the specific features of the various processing sectors and the specific needs of micro, small and medium-sized enterprises.

2. Associations and other bodies representing categories of controllers or processors may prepare codes of conduct, or amend or extend such codes, for the purpose of specifying the application of this Regulation, such as with regard to:

   a. fair and transparent processing;

   b. the legitimate interests pursued by controllers in specific contexts;

   c. the collection of personal data;

   d. the pseudonymisation of personal data;

   e. the information provided to the public and to data subjects;

   f. the exercise of the rights of data subjects;

   g. the information provided to, and the protection of, children, and the manner in which the consent of the holders of parental responsibility over children is to be obtained;

   h. the measures and procedures referred to in Articles 24 and 25 and the measures to ensure security of processing referred to in Article 32;

4

i.   the notification of personal data breaches to supervisory authority and the communication of such personal data breaches to data subjects;

j.   the transfer of personal data to third countries or international organisations; or

k.   out-of-court proceedings and other dispute resolution procedures for resolving disputes between controllers and data subjects with regard to processing, without prejudice to the rights of data subjects pursuant to Articles 77 and 79.

3.   In addition to adherence by controllers or processors subject to this Regulation, codes of conduct approved pursuant to paragraph 5 of this Article and having general validity pursuant to paragraph 9 of this Article may also be adhered to by controllers or processors that are not subject to this Regulation pursuant to Article 3 in order to provide appropriate safeguards within the framework of personal data transfers to third countries or international organisations under the terms referred to in point (e) of Article 46(2). Such controllers or processors shall make binding and enforceable commitments, via contractual or other legally binding instruments, to apply those appropriate safeguards including with regard to the rights of data subjects.

4.   A code of conduct referred to in paragraph 2 of this Article shall contain mechanisms which enable the body referred to in Article 41(1) to carry out the mandatory monitoring of compliance with its provisions by the controllers or processors which undertake to apply it, without prejudice to the tasks and powers of supervisory authority competent pursuant to Article 55 or 56.

5. Associations and other bodies referred to in paragraph 2 of this Article which intend to prepare a code of conduct or to amend or extend an existing code shall submit the draft code, amendment or extension to the supervisory authority which is competent pursuant to Article 55. The supervisory authority shall provide an opinion on whether the draft code, amendment or extension complies with this Regulation and shall approve that draft code, amendment or extension if it finds that it provides sufficient appropriate safeguards.

6. Where the draft code, or amendment or extension is approved in accordance with paragraph 5, and where the code of conduct concerned does not relate to processing activities in several Member States, the supervisory authority shall register and publish the code.

7. Where a draft code of conduct relates to processing activities in several Member States, the supervisory authority which is competent pursuant to Article 55 shall, before approving the draft code, amendment or extension, submit it in the procedure referred to in Article 63 to the Board which shall provide an opinion on whether the draft code, amendment or extension complies with this Regulation or, in the situation referred to in paragraph 3 of this Article, provides appropriate safeguards.

8. Where the opinion referred to in paragraph 7 confirms that the draft code, amendment or extension complies with this Regulation, or, in the situation referred to in paragraph 3, provides appropriate safeguards, the Board shall submit its opinion to the Commission.

9. The Commission may, by way of implementing acts, decide that the approved code of conduct, amendment or extension submitted to it pursuant to paragraph 8 of this Article have general validity within the Union. Those implementing acts shall be adopted in accordance with the examination procedure set out in Article 93(2).

4

10. The Commission shall ensure appropriate publicity for the approved codes which have been decided as having general validity in accordance with paragraph 9.

11. The Board shall collate all approved codes of conduct, amendments and extensions in a register and shall make them publicly available by way of appropriate means.

Easy Peasy Summary

- Member States, supervisory authorities, the European Data Protection Board, and the European Commission should all encourage organisations to create codes of conduct that will help them comply with GDPR Regulations.

- Associations and data privacy bodies can create or modify codes of conduct to help organisations meet the obligations described in the Regulation. These codes can include guidance on topics such as:

  o Fair and clear processing of personal information;

  o Legitimate interests companies have in specific contexts;

  o Proper collection of personal data;

  o Anonymising data;

  o Providing information to the public and data subjects;

  o Exercising rights of data subjects;

  o Protecting children's information when needed;

  o Online security measures for processing data;

  o Notifying supervisory authorities about personal data breaches and communicating with affected data subjects;

- o Transferring personal data to third countries or international organisations;

- o Providing out of court procedures for resolving disputes between controllers and data subjects.

- Controllers and processors subject to the Regulation should adhere to approved codes of conduct, as well as organisations that are not subject to GDPR. They must make binding and enforceable commitments (through legal agreements or other legally binding instruments) to comply with the appropriate safeguards set out in the Regulation.

- Codes of conduct must include mechanisms that enable the monitoring of adherence from organisations who have agreed to follow the code, without interfering with the responsibilities and powers of the supervisory authorities.

- Associations and other bodies must submit their draft code, an amendment, or an extension to the competent supervisory authority.

- The supervisory authority will give an opinion on whether the code, amendment, or extension complies with the Regulation and will approve it if it provides sufficient appropriate safeguards.

- If the draft code, amendment, or extension is approved and only applies to processing activities in one Member State, the supervisory authority will register and publish it.

- Before the supervisory authority approves a draft code, amendment, or extension that relates to processing activities in multiple Member States, it must ask the Board for an opinion.

- The Board will then provide an opinion on whether the code, amendment, or extension complies with the Regulation and whether it provides sufficient appropriate safeguards.

4

- If the opinion of the Board confirms that the draft code, amendment, or extension complies with the Regulation or provides adequate safeguards, it will submit its opinion to the Commission.

These decisions will be made in accordance with the examination procedure.

- The Commission can decide that the approved code of conduct, amendment, or extension has general validity throughout the Union.

- These decisions will be made in accordance with the examination procedure.

- The Commission will ensure appropriate publicity for the approved codes that have been decided to have general validity.

- The Board will compile all approved codes of conduct, amendments and extensions in a register and make them available to the public.

Article 41

Monitoring of Approved Codes of Conduct

Official GDPR Text

1. Without prejudice to the tasks and powers of the competent supervisory authority under Articles 57 and 58, the monitoring of compliance with a code of conduct pursuant to Article 40 may be carried out by a body which has an appropriate level of expertise in relation to the subject-matter of the code and is accredited for that purpose by the competent supervisory authority.

2. A body as referred to in paragraph 1 may be accredited to monitor compliance with a code of conduct where that body has:

   a. demonstrated its independence and expertise in relation to the subject-matter of the code to the satisfaction of the competent supervisory authority;

   b. established procedures which allow it to assess the eligibility of controllers and processors concerned to apply the code, to monitor their compliance with its provisions and to periodically review its operation;

   c. established procedures and structures to handle complaints about infringements of the code or the manner in which the code has been, or is being, implemented by a controller or processor, and to make those procedures and structures transparent to data subjects and the public; and

   d. demonstrated to the satisfaction of the competent supervisory authority that its tasks and duties do not result in a conflict of interests.

4

3. The competent supervisory authority shall submit the draft requirements for accreditation of a body as referred to in paragraph 1 of this Article to the Board pursuant to the consistency mechanism referred to in Article 63.

4. Without prejudice to the tasks and powers of the competent supervisory authority and the provisions of Chapter VIII, a body as referred to in paragraph 1 of this Article shall, subject to appropriate safeguards, take appropriate action in cases of infringement of the code by a controller or processor, including suspension or exclusion of the controller or processor concerned from the code. It shall inform the competent supervisory authority of such actions and the reasons for taking them.

5. The competent supervisory authority shall revoke the accreditation of a body as referred to in paragraph 1 if the conditions for accreditation are not, or are no longer, met or where actions taken by the body infringe this Regulation.

6. This Article shall not apply to processing carried out by public authorities and bodies.

Easy Peasy Summary

- A body with an appropriate level of expertise in the subject-matter of the code can be accredited to monitor compliance with it.

- They must:

  - be independent and demonstrate their expertise;

  - set up procedures for assessing eligibility and monitoring compliance with the code;

  - set up procedures for handling complaints about infringements;

  - demonstrate there is no conflict of interest; and

  - make those procedures transparent.

- The supervisory authority must approve the requirements for accreditation before submitting them to the Board.

- The body can take action against controllers or processors who violate the code and inform the supervisory authority of their actions and its reasons.

- Accreditation can be revoked if requirements are not met or if actions taken by the body infringe this Regulation.

- This Article does not apply to processing by public authorities and bodies.

This article does not apply to processing by public authorities and bodies.

4

Article 42
Certification

Official GDPR Text

1. The Member States, the supervisory authority, the Board and the Commission shall encourage, in particular at Union level, the establishment of data protection certification mechanisms and of data protection seals and marks, for the purpose of demonstrating compliance with this Regulation of processing operations by controllers and processors. The specific needs of micro, small and medium-sized enterprises shall be taken into account.

2. In addition to adherence by controllers or processors subject to this Regulation, data protection certification mechanisms, seals or marks approved pursuant to paragraph 5 of this Article may be established for the purpose of demonstrating the existence of appropriate safeguards provided by controllers or processors that are not subject to this Regulation pursuant to Article 3 within the framework of personal data transfers to third countries or international organisations under the terms referred to in point (f) of Article 46(2). Such controllers or processors shall make binding and enforceable commitments, via contractual or other legally binding instruments, to apply those appropriate safeguards, including with regard to the rights of data subjects.

3. The certification shall be voluntary and available via a process that is transparent.

4. A certification pursuant to this Article does not reduce the responsibility of the controller or the processor for compliance with this Regulation and is without prejudice to the tasks and powers of the supervisory authority which are competent pursuant to Article 55 or 56.

5. A certification pursuant to this Article shall be issued by the certification bodies referred to in Article 43 or by the competent supervisory authority, on the basis of criteria approved by that competent supervisory authority pursuant to Article 58(3) or by the Board pursuant to Article 63. Where the criteria are approved by the Board, this may result in a common certification, the European Data Protection Seal.

6. The controller or processor which submits its processing to the certification mechanism shall provide the certification body referred to in Article 43, or where applicable, the competent supervisory authority, with all information and access to its processing activities which are necessary to conduct the certification procedure.

7. Certification shall be issued to a controller or processor for a maximum period of three years and may be renewed, under the same conditions, provided that the relevant requirements continue to be met. Certification shall be withdrawn, as applicable, by the certification bodies referred to in Article 43 or by the competent supervisory authority where the requirements for the certification are not or are no longer met.

8. The Board shall collate all certification mechanisms and data protection seals and marks in a register and shall make them publicly available by any appropriate means.

4

Easy Peasy Summary

- Member States, the supervisory authorities, the Board and the Commission will promote data protection certification mechanisms, seals and marks at a Union level to show compliance with this Regulation of processing operations by controllers and processors.

- They should take into account the specific needs of smaller businesses.

- They can also be established for organisations that are not subject to this Regulation.

- Those organisations must make binding commitments through contractual or other legally binding instruments to apply appropriate safeguards concerning data subjects' rights.

Certification is voluntary and must be achieved via a transparent process.

- Certification is voluntary and must be achieved via a transparent process.

- Certification does not reduce a controller or processor's responsibility for compliance with this Regulation and does not affect the tasks and powers of the competent supervisory authority.

- It must be issued by certification bodies referred to in Article 43 or the competent supervisory authority, based on criteria approved by the latter.

- The controller or processor must provide all necessary information and access for the certification procedure.

- Certification is valid for up to three years and may be renewed if criteria are still met. It can be withdrawn if criteria are not or are no longer met.

- The Board will record all certification mechanisms, seals and marks in a register available to the public.

Article 43

Certification Bodies

Official GDPR Text

1. Without prejudice to the tasks and powers of the competent supervisory authority under Articles 57 and 58, certification bodies which have an appropriate level of expertise in relation to data protection shall, after informing the supervisory authority in order to allow it to exercise its powers pursuant to point (h) of Article 58(2) where necessary, issue and renew certification. Member States shall ensure that those certification bodies are accredited by one or both of the following:

    a. the supervisory authority which is competent pursuant to Article 55 or 56;

    b. the national accreditation body named in accordance with Regulation (EC) No 765/2008 of the European Parliament and of the Council[1] in accordance with EN-ISO/IEC 17065/2012 and with the additional requirements established by the supervisory authority which is competent pursuant to Article 55 or 56.

2. Certification bodies referred to in paragraph 1 shall be accredited in accordance with that paragraph only where they have:

    a. demonstrated their independence and expertise in relation to the subject-matter of the certification to the satisfaction of the competent supervisory authority;

    b. undertaken to respect the criteria referred to in Article 42(5) and approved by the supervisory authority which is competent pursuant to Article 55 or 56 or by the Board pursuant to Article 63;

c. established procedures for the issuing, periodic review and withdrawal of data protection certification, seals and marks;

d. established procedures and structures to handle complaints about infringements of the certification or the manner in which the certification has been, or is being, implemented by the controller or processor, and to make those procedures and structures transparent to data subjects and the public; and

e. demonstrated, to the satisfaction of the competent supervisory authority, that their tasks and duties do not result in a conflict of interests.

3. The accreditation of certification bodies as referred to in paragraphs 1 and 2 of this Article shall take place on the basis of criteria approved by the supervisory authority which is competent pursuant to Article 55 or 56 or by the Board pursuant to Article 63. In the case of accreditation pursuant to point (b) of paragraph 1 of this Article, those requirements shall complement those envisaged in Regulation (EC) No 765/2008 and the technical rules that describe the methods and procedures of the certification bodies.

4. The certification bodies referred to in paragraph 1 shall be responsible for the proper assessment leading to the certification or the withdrawal of such certification without prejudice to the responsibility of the controller or processor for compliance with this Regulation. The accreditation shall be issued for a maximum period of five years and may be renewed on the same conditions provided that the certification body meets the requirements set out in this Article.

5. The certification bodies referred to in paragraph 1 shall provide the competent supervisory authority with the reasons for granting or withdrawing the requested certification.

6. The requirements referred to in paragraph 3 of this Article and the criteria referred to in Article 42(5) shall be made public by the supervisory authority in an easily accessible form. The supervisory authority shall also transmit those requirements and criteria to the Board. The Board shall collate all certification mechanisms and data protection seals in a register and shall make them publicly available by any appropriate means.

7. Without prejudice to Chapter VIII, the competent supervisory authority or the national accreditation body shall revoke an accreditation of a certification body pursuant to paragraph 1 of this Article where the conditions for the accreditation are not, or are no longer, met or where actions taken by a certification body infringe this Regulation.

8. The Commission shall be empowered to adopt delegated acts in accordance with Article 92 for the purpose of specifying the requirements to be taken into account for the data protection certification mechanisms referred to in Article 42(1).

9. The Commission may adopt implementing acts laying down technical standards for certification mechanisms and data protection seals and marks, and mechanisms to promote and recognise those certification mechanisms, seals and marks. Those implementing acts shall be adopted in accordance with the examination procedure referred to in Article 93(2).

4

Easy Peasy Summary

- Certifications must be issued by certification bodies with an appropriate level of data protection expertise.

- Member States should ensure such certification bodies are accredited by either the competent supervisory authority or the national accreditation body, in accordance with EN-ISO/IEC 17065/2012 and any additional requirements from the relevant supervisory authority.

- This is without prejudice to the tasks and powers of the competent supervisory authority.

- The certification bodies shall be accredited by a supervisory authority, a national accreditation body or both.

- Certification bodies must:

  o demonstrate independence and expertise related to the certification;

  o agree to respect the criteria approved by the competent supervisory authority or the Board;

  o have processes for issuing, reviewing and withdrawing certifications, seals and marks;

  o have procedures for handling complaints about violations of certification implementation; and

  o demonstrate there is no conflict of interest.

- Accreditation of certification bodies must be done on the basis of requirements approved by the competent supervisory authority or the Board.

- The accreditation requirements should complement those outlined in Regulation (EC) No 765/2008 and there should be technical rules explaining the certification body's methods and procedures.

- Certification bodies are responsible for assessing the certification or withdrawal of it, without reducing the controller's or processor's responsibility for complying with the Regulation.

- Certification can be valid for up to five years. They can be renewed if the certification body meets the requirements in this Article.

Certification can be valid for up to five years.

- Certification bodies must provide the competent supervisory authorities with reasons for granting or withdrawing certification.

- The requirements and criteria must be made public by the supervisory authority in an easily accessible way. The supervisory authority must also share them with the Board, which will collate all certification mechanisms and seals in a public register.

- The accreditation of a certification body can be revoked by either the competent supervisory authority or national accreditation body if:

  - the conditions for accreditation are not met; or

  - the conditions are no longer being met; or

  - the certification body took actions that violate the Regulation.

- The Commission has the power to adopt delegated acts specifying the requirements for data protection certification mechanisms.

- The Commission can adopt implementing acts laying down technical standards for certification mechanisms and data protection seals and marks, as well as mechanisms to promote and recognise them.

- These implementing acts will be adopted through the examination procedure.

4

5

Transfers of Personal Data to Third Countries or International Organisations

Article 44
General Principle for Transfers

Official GDPR Text

Any transfer of personal data which are undergoing processing or are intended for processing after transfer to a third country or to an international organisation shall take place only if, subject to the other provisions of this Regulation, the conditions laid down in this Chapter are complied with by the controller and processor, including for onward transfers of personal data from the third country or an international organisation to another third country or to another international organisation. All provisions in this Chapter shall be applied in order to ensure that the level of protection of natural persons guaranteed by this Regulation is not undermined.

Easy Peasy Summary

- Personal data transfers to a third country or international organisation are only allowed if the controller or processor comply with the conditions in this Chapter of the Regulation.

- These conditions must be met to make sure that the level of protection remains consistent with this Regulation.

Article 45

Transfers on the Basis of an Adequacy Decision

Official GDPR Text

1. A transfer of personal data to a third country or an international organisation may take place where the Commission has decided that the third country, a territory or one or more specified sectors within that third country, or the international organisation in question ensures an adequate level of protection. Such a transfer shall not require any specific authorisation.

2. When assessing the adequacy of the level of protection, the Commission shall, in particular, take account of the following elements:

   a. the rule of law, respect for human rights and fundamental freedoms, relevant legislation, both general and sectoral, including concerning public security, defence, national security and criminal law and the access of public authorities to personal data, as well as the implementation of such legislation, data protection rules, professional rules and security measures, including rules for the onward transfer of personal data to another third country or international organisation which are complied with in that country or international organisation, case-law, as well as effective and enforceable data subject rights and effective administrative and judicial redress for the data subjects whose personal data are being transferred;

5

b. the existence and effective functioning of one or more independent supervisory authorities in the third country or to which an international organisation is subject, with responsibility for ensuring and enforcing compliance with the data protection rules, including adequate enforcement powers, for assisting and advising the data subjects in exercising their rights and for cooperation with the supervisory authorities of the Member States; and

c. the international commitments the third country or international organisation concerned has entered into, or other obligations arising from legally binding conventions or instruments as well as from its participation in multilateral or regional systems, in particular in relation to the protection of personal data.

3. The Commission, after assessing the adequacy of the level of protection, may decide, by means of implementing act, that a third country, a territory or one or more specified sectors within a third country, or an international organisation ensures an adequate level of protection within the meaning of paragraph 2 of this Article. The implementing act shall provide for a mechanism for a periodic review, at least every four years, which shall take into account all relevant developments in the third country or international organisation. The implementing act shall specify its territorial and sectoral application and, where applicable, identify the supervisory authority or authorities referred to in point (b) of paragraph 2 of this Article. The implementing act shall be adopted in accordance with the examination procedure referred to in Article 93(2).

4. The Commission shall, on an ongoing basis, monitor developments in third countries and international organisations that could affect the functioning of decisions adopted pursuant to paragraph 3 of this Article and decisions adopted on the basis of Article 25(6) of Directive 95/46/EC.

5. The Commission shall, where available information reveals, in particular following the review referred to in paragraph 3 of this Article, that a third country, a territory or one or more specified sectors within a third country, or an international organisation no longer ensures an adequate level of protection within the meaning of paragraph 2 of this Article, to the extent necessary, repeal, amend or suspend the decision referred to in paragraph 3 of this Article by means of implementing acts without retro-active effect. Those implementing acts shall be adopted in accordance with the examination procedure referred to in Article 93(2). On duly justified imperative grounds of urgency, the Commission shall adopt immediately applicable implementing acts in accordance with the procedure referred to in Article 93(3).

5

6. The Commission shall enter into consultations with the third country or international organisation with a view to remedying the situation giving rise to the decision made pursuant to paragraph 5.

7. A decision pursuant to paragraph 5 of this Article is without prejudice to transfers of personal data to the third country, a territory or one or more specified sectors within that third country, or the international organisation in question pursuant to Articles 46 to 49.

8. The Commission shall publish in the Official Journal of the European Union and on its website a list of the third countries, territories and specified sectors within a third country and international organisations for which it has decided that an adequate level of protection is or is no longer ensured.

9. Decisions adopted by the Commission on the basis of Article 25(6) of Directive 95/46/EC shall remain in force until amended, replaced or repealed by a Commission Decision adopted in accordance with paragraph 3 or 5 of this Article.

Easy Peasy Summary

- Transfers of personal data to a third country or to an international organisation are allowed if the European Commission has decided that the country, territory, sector-specific area, or organisation in question provides adequate protection for individuals.

No specific authorisation is required for such transfer.

- No specific authorisation is required for such transfers.

- When considering the adequacy of data protection, the Commission will take into account:

  - the rule of law;

  - respect for human rights and fundamental freedoms;

  - relevant national legislation (concerning public security, defence, and criminal law) and implementation of that legislation;

  - data protection rules;

  - professional rules;

  - security measures;

  - rules for onward transfer to another third country or organisation;

  - independent supervisory authorities in the third country or international organisation with responsibility for enforcing data protection rules and assisting/advising data subjects in exercising their rights; and

  - international commitments entered into by the third country or international organisation concerning data protection.

- The Commission may decide, through an implementing act, that a third country, territory or sector-specific area, or international organisation provides adequate data protection based on the assessment of the level of protection.

- This implementing act should provide for a periodic review every 4 years and specify its territorial and sectoral application as well as any relevant supervisory authorities.

- This decision is to be made by following the examination procedure. The Commission will continuously monitor developments in third countries and international organisations which could have an effect on its decisions.

- The Commission can repeal, modify, or suspend a decision if information comes to light that shows that a third country, territory, sector-specific area, or international organisation does not provide adequate data protection.

5

- These changes will be made through implementing acts without creating any retro-active effect and must also follow the examination procedure.

- The Commission can take immediate action in necessary, urgent circumstances.

- The Commission must consult with the third country or international organisation to address the issue.

The Commission can take immediate action in necessary, urgent circumstances.

- The decision to repeal, suspend or amend the approval of adequate level of protection will not affect data transfers that use:

  o Binding Corporate Rules (BCR);

  o standard data protection clauses adopted by the Commission;

  o standard data protection clauses adopted by a supervisory authority and approved by the Commission;

- o an approved code of conduct; and

- o an approved certification mechanism.

- The Commission will publish a list of third countries, territories, specified sectors and international organisations which have an adequate or inadequate level of protection in the European Union Official Journal and website.

- Any decisions adopted by the Commission will continue to be valid until changed or revoked by a Commission decision.

Article 46

Transfers Subject to Appropriate Safeguards

Official GDPR Text

1. In the absence of a decision pursuant to Article 45(3), a controller or processor may transfer personal data to a third country or an international organisation only if the controller or processor has provided appropriate safeguards, and on condition that enforceable data subject rights and effective legal remedies for data subjects are available.

2. The appropriate safeguards referred to in paragraph 1 may be provided for, without requiring any specific authorisation from a supervisory authority, by:

    a. a legally binding and enforceable instrument between public authorities or bodies;

    b. binding corporate rules in accordance with Article 47;

    c. standard data protection clauses adopted by the Commission in accordance with the examination procedure referred to in Article 93(2);

    d. standard data protection clauses adopted by a supervisory authority and approved by the Commission pursuant to the examination procedure referred to in Article 93(2);

    e. an approved code of conduct pursuant to Article 40 together with binding and enforceable commitments of the controller or processor in the third country to apply the appropriate safeguards, including as regards data subjects' rights; or

5

f.   an approved certification mechanism pursuant to Article 42 together with binding and enforceable commitments of the controller or processor in the third country to apply the appropriate safeguards, including as regards data subjects' rights.

3.   Subject to the authorisation from the competent supervisory authority, the appropriate safeguards referred to in paragraph 1 may also be provided for, in particular, by:

    a.   contractual clauses between the controller or processor and the controller, processor or the recipient of the personal data in the third country or international organisation; or

    b.   provisions to be inserted into administrative arrangements between public authorities or bodies which include enforceable and effective data subject rights.

4.   The supervisory authority shall apply the consistency mechanism referred to in Article 63 in the cases referred to in paragraph 3 of this Article.

5.   Authorisations by a Member State or supervisory authority on the basis of Article 26(2) of Directive 95/46/EC shall remain valid until amended, replaced or repealed, if necessary, by that supervisory authority. Decisions adopted by the Commission on the basis of Article 26(4) of Directive 95/46/EC shall remain in force until amended, replaced or repealed, if necessary, by a Commission Decision adopted in accordance with paragraph 2 of this Article.

Easy Peasy Summary

- Where a country or international organisation has not been listed as providing an adequate level of data protection, a controller or processor can only transfer personal there if:

  o the right safeguards are in place, and

  o data subjects have enforceable rights; and

  o effective legal remedies exist.

- The appropriate safeguards can be put in place without needing any specific authorisation from a supervisory authority. This can be done by:

  o a legally binding agreement between authorities;

  o Binding Corporate Rules (BCR);

  o standard data protection clauses adopted by the Commission;

  o standard data protection clauses adopted by a supervisory authority and approved by the Commission;

  o an approved code of conduct;

  o an approved certification mechanism.

... a controller or processor can only transfer personal data there if the right safeguards are in place ...

5

Article 47

Binding Corporate Rules

Official GDPR Text

1. The competent supervisory authority shall approve binding corporate rules in accordance with the consistency mechanism set out in Article 63, provided that they:

   a. are legally binding and apply to and are enforced by every member concerned of the group of undertakings, or group of enterprises engaged in a joint economic activity, including their employees;

   b. expressly confer enforceable rights on data subjects with regard to the processing of their personal data; and

   c. fulfil the requirements laid down in paragraph 2.

2. The binding corporate rules referred to in paragraph 1 shall specify at least:

   a. the structure and contact details of the group of undertakings, or group of enterprises engaged in a joint economic activity and of each of its members;

   b. the data transfers or set of transfers, including the categories of personal data, the type of processing and its purposes, the type of data subjects affected and the identification of the third country or countries in question;

   c. their legally binding nature, both internally and externally;

   d. the application of the general data protection principles, in particular purpose limitation, data minimisation, limited storage periods, data quality, data protection by design and by default, legal basis for processing, processing of special categories of personal data, measures to ensure data security, and the requirements in respect of onward transfers to bodies not bound by the binding corporate rules;

e. the rights of data subjects in regard to processing and the means to exercise those rights, including the right not to be subject to decisions based solely on automated processing, including profiling in accordance with Article 22, the right to lodge a complaint with the competent supervisory authority and before the competent courts of the Member States in accordance with Article 79, and to obtain redress and, where appropriate, compensation for a breach of the binding corporate rules;

f. the acceptance by the controller or processor established on the territory of a Member State of liability for any breaches of the binding corporate rules by any member concerned not established in the Union; the controller or the processor shall be exempt from that liability, in whole or in part, only if it proves that that member is not responsible for the event giving rise to the damage;

g. how the information on the binding corporate rules, in particular on the provisions referred to in points (d), (e) and (f) of this paragraph, is provided to the data subjects in addition to Articles 13 and 14;

h. the tasks of any data protection officer designated in accordance with Article 37 or any other person or entity in charge of the monitoring compliance with the binding corporate rules within the group of undertakings, or group of enterprises engaged in a joint economic activity, as well as monitoring training and complaint-handling;

i. the complaint procedures;

j. the mechanisms within the group of undertakings, or group of enterprises engaged in a joint economic activity for ensuring the verification of compliance with the binding

5

corporate rules. Such mechanisms shall include data protection audits and methods for ensuring corrective actions to protect the rights of the data subject. Results of such verification should be communicated to the person or entity referred to in point (h) and to the board of the controlling undertaking of a group of undertakings, or of the group of enterprises engaged in a joint economic activity, and should be available upon request to the competent supervisory authority;

k. the mechanisms for reporting and recording changes to the rules and reporting those changes to the supervisory authority;

l. the cooperation mechanism with the supervisory authority to ensure compliance by any member of the group of undertakings, or group of enterprises engaged in a joint economic activity, in particular by making available to the supervisory authority the results of verifications of the measures referred to in point (j);

m. the mechanisms for reporting to the competent supervisory authority any legal requirements to which a member of the group of undertakings, or group of enterprises engaged in a joint economic activity is subject in a third country which are likely to have a substantial adverse effect on the guarantees provided by the binding corporate rules; and

n. the appropriate data protection training to personnel having permanent or regular access to personal data.

3. The Commission may specify the format and procedures for the exchange of information between controllers, processors and supervisory authority for binding corporate rules within the meaning of this Article. Those implementing acts shall be adopted in accordance with the examination procedure set out in Article 93(2).

Easy Peasy Summary

- Binding Corporate Rules (BCR) will be approved by a supervisory authority as long as they:

  o are legally binding;

  o apply to and are enforced by every part of the corporate group including their employees;

  o allow data subjects to enjoy their data subject rights; and

  o fulfil the below requirements.

- Binding Corporate Rules must specify:

  o the structure of the corporate group and each of its members;

  o the contact details of the corporate group and each of its members;

  o data transfers or set of transfers including categories of personal data, the types of processing, the purposes of processing, the types of data subjects affected, the details of third countries in question;

  o they are legally binding internally and externally;

  o application of general data protection principles – purpose limitation, data minimisation, limited storage period, data quality, data protection by design/default, legal basis for processing of special categories of personal data, measures to ensure data security for onward transfers to any organisation or person not bound by the BCR;

  o the rights of data subjects and how those rights can be exercised;

Binding Corporate Rules must specify ... they are legally binding internally and externally ...

5

- that the controller or processor that is established in the Member State accepts liability for any breaches of BCR by any member of the group that is not based in the European Union;

- how data subjects will be given information about the BCR;

- the tasks of any data protection officer or any person in charge of monitoring compliance with the BCR;

- complaint procedures;

- what mechanisms are in place to verify the BCR are being followed;

- what mechanisms are in place for reporting and recording changes to the rules;

- how changes will be reported to the supervisory authority;

- the cooperation mechanism with supervisory authority to ensure compliance;

- the mechanism for reporting any legal requirements in any third country which could have a severe negative on the guarantees provided by the BCR (to the supervisory authority); and

- what data protection training will be delivered to personnel that have access to personal data.

- The Commission can specify the format and procedures for how communications should take place between controllers, processors and supervisory authorities for the BCR.

Article 48

Transfers or Disclosures Not Authorised by Union Law

Official GDPR Text

Any judgment of a court or tribunal and any decision of an administrative authority of a third country requiring a controller or processor to transfer or disclose personal data may only be recognised or enforceable in any manner if based on an international agreement, such as a mutual legal assistance treaty, in force between the requesting third country and the Union or a Member State, without prejudice to other grounds for transfer pursuant to this Chapter.

5

Easy Peasy Summary

A judgment by a court (or administrative authority) in a third country to transfer or share personal data, is only enforceable where an international agreement is in place.

Article 49

Derogations for Specific Situations

Official GDPR Text

1. In the absence of an adequacy decision pursuant to Article 45(3), or of appropriate safeguards pursuant to Article 46, including binding corporate rules, a transfer or a set of transfers of personal data to a third country or an international organisation shall take place only on one of the following conditions:

    a. the data subject has explicitly consented to the proposed transfer, after having been informed of the possible risks of such transfers for the data subject due to the absence of an adequacy decision and appropriate safeguards;

    b. the transfer is necessary for the performance of a contract between the data subject and the controller or the implementation of pre-contractual measures taken at the data subject's request;

    c. the transfer is necessary for the conclusion or performance of a contract concluded in the interest of the data subject between the controller and another natural or legal person;

    d. the transfer is necessary for important reasons of public interest;

    e. the transfer is necessary for the establishment, exercise or defence of legal claims;

    f. the transfer is necessary in order to protect the vital interests of the data subject or of other persons, where the data subject is physically or legally incapable of giving consent;

g. the transfer is made from a register which according to Union or Member State law is intended to provide information to the public and which is open to consultation either by the public in general or by any person who can demonstrate a legitimate interest, but only to the extent that the conditions laid down by Union or Member State law for consultation are fulfilled in the particular case.

Where a transfer could not be based on a provision in Article 45 or 46, including the provisions on binding corporate rules, and none of the derogations for a specific situation referred to in the first subparagraph of this paragraph is applicable, a transfer to a third country or an international organisation may take place only if the transfer is not repetitive, concerns only a limited number of data subjects, is necessary for the purposes of compelling legitimate interests pursued by the controller which are not overridden by the interests or rights and freedoms of the data subject, and the controller has assessed all the circumstances surrounding the data transfer and has on the basis of that assessment provided suitable safeguards with regard to the protection of personal data. The controller shall inform the supervisory authority of the transfer. The controller shall, in addition to providing the information referred to in Articles 13 and 14, inform the data subject of the transfer and on the compelling legitimate interests pursued.

2. A transfer pursuant to point (g) of the first subparagraph of paragraph 1 shall not involve the entirety of the personal data or entire categories of the personal data contained in the register. Where the register is intended for consultation by persons having a legitimate interest, the transfer shall be made only at the request of those persons or if they are to be the recipients.

3. Points (a), (b) and (c) of the first subparagraph of paragraph 1 and the second subparagraph thereof shall not apply to activities carried out by public authorities in the exercise of their public powers.

5

4. The public interest referred to in point (d) of the first subparagraph of paragraph 1 shall be recognised in Union law or in the law of the Member State to which the controller is subject.

5. In the absence of an adequacy decision, Union or Member State law may, for important reasons of public interest, expressly set limits to the transfer of specific categories of personal data to a third country or an international organisation. Member States shall notify such provisions to the Commission.

6. The controller or processor shall document the assessment as well as the suitable safeguards referred to in the second subparagraph of paragraph 1 of this Article in the records referred to in Article 30.

Easy Peasy Summary

*   Where there is no adequacy decision or appropriate safeguards in place, a transfer of personal data to a third country (or organisation) can only take place if:

    o   the data subject has given explicit consent to such transfer after being informed about the risk;

    o   the transfer is required for the performance of the contract between the controller and the data subject (or for pre-contractual stages);

    o   the transfer is required for the conclusion or performance of a contract between the controller and other natural or legal person and the conclusion is in the interest of the data subject;

    o   the transfer is in the public interest;

- the transfer is necessary in relation to a legal claim;

- the transfer is required to keep someone alive;

- the information is in a public register (subject to meeting the conditions set by the register owner).

- Where there is no adequacy decision, no appropriate safeguards, and none of the above conditions apply, then a transfer can only take place if:

  - it is not repetitive but a one-off;

  - it only concerns a small number of data subjects;

  - it is necessary because of the legitimate interest of the controller and on balance does not infringe too much on the data subjects rights and freedoms; and

  - the controller has looked at everything around the transfer and can put in place measures to keep the personal data secure and private.

In this case, the controller must inform:

... the controller must inform the supervisory authority of the transfer ...

  - the supervisory authority of the transfer; and

  - the data subject that the transfer is taking place and what the controller's legitimate interest is.

- A transfer mentioned in paragraph 1, point (g), should not involve all data in the register. It should only occur if requested by or intended for people with a legitimate interest.

- Paragraph 1's points (a), (b), and (c), along with its second subparagraph, do not apply to activities performed by public authorities while exercising their public powers.

- The public interest in paragraph 1, point (d) must be recognized in either Union law or the controller's local law.

5

The controller or processor should keep a record of the assessment and safeguards ...

- Without an adequacy decision, Union or Member State law can limit the transfer of specific personal data types to a third country or international organisation for public interest reasons. Member States must inform the Commission of such rules.

- The controller or processor should keep a record of the assessment and safeguards mentioned in paragraph 1, second subparagraph, in the records described in Article 30.

Article 50

International Cooperation for the Protection of Personal Data

Official GDPR Text

In relation to third countries and international organisations, the Commission and supervisory authorities shall take appropriate steps to:

a. develop international cooperation mechanisms to facilitate the effective enforcement of legislation for the protection of personal data;

b. provide international mutual assistance in the enforcement of legislation for the protection of personal data, including through notification, complaint referral, investigative assistance and information exchange, subject to appropriate safeguards for the protection of personal data and other fundamental rights and freedoms;

c. engage relevant stakeholders in discussion and activities aimed at furthering international cooperation in the enforcement of legislation for the protection of personal data;

d. promote the exchange and documentation of personal data protection legislation and practice, including on jurisdictional conflicts with third countries.

5

Easy Peasy Summary

- The Commission and supervisory authority must do their best to cooperate with third countries and international organisations.

- International cooperation should be developed to protect personal data and enforce laws effectively.

- International mutual assistance should be provided to enforce laws to protect personal data, rights and freedoms.

Data protection laws and practices should be promoted by sharing documents.

- Stakeholders should be engaged in discussions and activities to further promote international cooperation for the protection of personal data.

- Data protection laws and practices should be promoted by sharing documents.

6

Independent Supervisory Authorities

Article 51

Supervisory Authority

Official GDPR Text

1. Each Member State shall provide for one or more independent public authorities to be responsible for monitoring the application of this Regulation, in order to protect the fundamental rights and freedoms of natural persons in relation to processing and to facilitate the free flow of personal data within the Union ('supervisory authority').

2. Each supervisory authority shall contribute to the consistent application of this Regulation throughout the Union. For that purpose, the supervisory authorities shall cooperate with each other and the Commission in accordance with Chapter VII.

3. Where more than one supervisory authority is established in a Member State, that Member State shall designate the supervisory authority which is to represent those authorities in the Board and shall set out the mechanism to ensure compliance by the other authorities with the rules relating to the consistency mechanism referred to in Article 63.

4. Each Member State shall notify to the Commission the provisions of its law which it adopts pursuant to this Chapter, by 25 May 2018 and, without delay, any subsequent amendment affecting them.

Easy Peasy Summary

- Each Member State must appoint at least one independent public authority to monitor the application of GDPR and protect the rights and freedoms of data subjects.

- These supervisory authorities will cooperate with each other and the Commission to make sure the Regulation is being applied consistently.

- Where a Member State has more than one supervisory authority, they should pick one to represent them in the Board. There should be a system for the other supervisory authorities to follow the consistency mechanism rules.

- Member States must notify the Commission if they adopt any law provisions, or make any changes related to this Chapter.

... must appoint at least one independent public authority to monitor the application of GDPR ...

6

Article 52

Independence

Official GDPR Text

1. Each supervisory authority shall act with complete independence in performing its tasks and exercising its powers in accordance with this Regulation.

2. The member or members of each supervisory authority shall, in the performance of their tasks and exercise of their powers in accordance with this Regulation, remain free from external influence, whether direct or indirect, and shall neither seek nor take instructions from anybody.

3. Member or members of each supervisory authority shall refrain from any action incompatible with their duties and shall not, during their term of office, engage in any incompatible occupation, whether gainful or not.

4. Each Member State shall ensure that each supervisory authority is provided with the human, technical and financial resources, premises and infrastructure necessary for the effective performance of its tasks and exercise of its powers, including those to be carried out in the context of mutual assistance, cooperation and participation in the Board.

5. Each Member State shall ensure that each supervisory authority chooses and has its own staff which shall be subject to the exclusive direction of the member or members of the supervisory authority concerned.

6. Each Member State shall ensure that each supervisory authority that it has separate, public annual budgets, which may be part of the overall state or national budget.

Easy Peasy Summary

Each supervisory authority must act independently.

- Each supervisory authority must act independently.

- No direct or indirect external influence is allowed.

- Anyone that works for a supervisory authority must stay away from any action that is incompatible with their duties and they are not allowed to engage in any such occupation during their term of office.

- Member States must provide the supervisory authority with:

    o necessary resources;

    o premises;

    o infrastructure;

    o staff;

    o an annual budget.

- Financial control over the supervisory authority must not affect its independence.

6

Article 53

General Conditions for the Members of the Supervisory Authority

Official GDPR Text

1. Member States shall provide for each member of their supervisory authorities to be appointed by means of a transparent procedure by:

    a. their parliament;

    b. their government;

    c. their head of State; or

    d. an independent body entrusted with the appointment under Member State law.

2. Each member shall have the qualifications, experience and skills, in particular in the area of the protection of personal data, required to perform its duties and exercise its powers.

3. The duties of a member shall end in the event of the expiry of the term of office, resignation or compulsory retirement, in accordance with the law of the Member State concerned.

4. A member shall be dismissed only in cases of serious misconduct or if the member no longer fulfils the conditions required for the performance of the duties.

Easy Peasy Summary

- Member States must appoint members of their supervisory authorities through a transparent process. This can be:

  o their Parliament;

  o their Government;

  o their Head of State;

  o an independent body.

- Members of the supervisory authorities must have the qualifications, experience, and skills necessary to perform their duties and exercise their powers.

- A member of the supervisory authorities duties end when:

  o their term has expired;

  o they resign; or

  o retirement is mandatory because of a Member State law.

- A member of the supervisory authorities can be dismissed for serious misconduct or if they no longer have the qualifications and skills required to perform their duties.

... must have the qualifications, experience, and skills necessary to perform their duties ...

6

Article 54

Rules on the Establishment of the Supervisory Authority

Official GDPR Text

1. Each Member State shall provide by law for all of the following:

    a. the establishment of each supervisory authority;

    b. the qualifications and eligibility conditions required to be appointed as member of each supervisory authority;

    c. the rules and procedures for the appointment of the member or members of each supervisory authority;

    d. the duration of the term of the member or members of each supervisory authority of no less than four years, except for the first appointment after 24 May 2016, part of which may take place for a shorter period where that is necessary to protect the independence of the supervisory authority by means of a staggered appointment procedure;

    e. whether and, if so, for how many terms the member or members of each supervisory authority is eligible for reappointment;

    f. the conditions governing the obligations of the member or members and staff of each supervisory authority, prohibitions on actions, occupations and benefits incompatible therewith during and after the term of office and rules governing the cessation of employment.

2. The member or members and the staff of each supervisory authority shall, in accordance with Union or Member State law, be subject to a duty of professional secrecy both during and after their term of office, with regard to any confidential information which has come to their knowledge in the course of the performance of their tasks or exercise of their powers. During their term of office, that duty of professional secrecy shall in particular apply to reporting by natural persons of infringements of this Regulation.

Easy Peasy Summary

- Each Member State must set up laws governing:

  - the formation of supervisory authorities;

  - qualifications needed for members;

  - rules and procedures around their appointment;

  - the duration the term (maximum 4 years);

  - potential re-appointment eligibility;

  - rules surrounding obligations, prohibitions, and benefits related to members and staff.

- Supervisory authorities members and staff are bound by professional secrecy (during and after their term). They also have a duty to report any breaches of this Regulation.

6

Supervisory authorities members and staff are bound by professional secrecy …

Article 55

Competence

Official GDPR Text

1. Each supervisory authority shall be competent for the performance of the tasks assigned to and the exercise of the powers conferred on it in accordance with this Regulation on the territory of its own Member State.

2. Where processing is carried out by public authorities or private bodies acting on the basis of point (c) or (e) of Article 6(1), the supervisory authority of the Member State concerned shall be competent. In such cases Article 56 does not apply.

3. Supervisory authorities shall not be competent to supervise processing operations of courts acting in their judicial capacity.

Easy Peasy Summary

... responsible for tasks and powers assigned to them within their own Member State.

- Each supervisory authority is responsible for tasks and powers assigned to them within their own Member State.

- Article 56 does not apply when processing is done by public authorities or private bodies to comply with a legal obligation or for performing a task in the public interest. Where this is the case, the competent supervisory authority is the supervisory authority of that Member State, such as CNIL in France or AEPD in Spain.

- Supervisory authorities are not to supervise any processing operations of courts acting in judicial capacities.

Article 56

Competence of the Lead Supervisory Authority

Official GDPR Text

1. Without prejudice to Article 55, the supervisory authority of the main establishment or of the single establishment of the controller or processor shall be competent to act as lead supervisory authority for the cross-border processing carried out by that controller or processor in accordance with the procedure provided in Article 60.

2. By derogation from paragraph 1, each supervisory authority shall be competent to handle a complaint lodged with it or a possible infringement of this Regulation, if the subject matter relates only to an establishment in its Member State or substantially affects data subjects only in its Member State.

3. In the cases referred to in paragraph 2 of this Article, the supervisory authority shall inform the lead supervisory authority without delay on that matter. Within a period of three weeks after being informed, the lead supervisory authority shall decide whether or not it will handle the case in accordance with the procedure provided in Article 60, taking into account whether or not there is an establishment of the controller or processor in the Member State of which the supervisory authority informed it.

4. Where the lead supervisory authority decides to handle the case, the procedure provided in Article 60 shall apply. The supervisory authority which informed the lead supervisory authority may submit to the lead supervisory authority a draft for a decision. The lead supervisory authority shall take utmost account of that draft when preparing the draft decision referred to in Article 60(3).

6

5. Where the lead supervisory authority decides not to handle the case, the supervisory authority which informed the lead supervisory authority shall handle it according to Articles 61 and 62.

6. The lead supervisory authority shall be the sole interlocutor of the controller or processor for the cross-border processing carried out by that controller or processor.

Easy Peasy Summary

Any complaints ... with this Regulation will be handled by the supervisory authority of the Member State where the incident took place.

- If the controller is processing data in more than one country, the supervisory authority of the member state in which the controller is based (or carries out most of the processing activity) will be the lead supervisory authority.

- Any complaints about non-compliance with this Regulation will be handled by the supervisory authority of the Member State where the incident took place.

- If the relevant supervisory authority is not the lead supervisory authority, it must report the incident to the lead supervisory authority.

- The lead supervisory authority then has 3 weeks to decide whether it will handle the incident or let the reporting supervisory authority handle it.

- When the lead supervisory authority handles a case, they follow Article 60. The informing authority can submit a draft decision, which the lead authority must consider carefully while creating their own draft decision.

- If the lead supervisory authority chooses not to handle the case, the informing authority will manage it following Articles 61 and 62.

- Where the controller is engaged in cross-border data processing, then the controller will only communicate with the lead supervisory authority.

Article 57

Tasks

Official GDPR Text

1. Without prejudice to other tasks set out under this Regulation, each supervisory authority shall on its territory:

    a. monitor and enforce the application of this Regulation;

    b. promote public awareness and understanding of the risks, rules, safeguards and rights in relation to processing. Activities addressed specifically to children shall receive specific attention;

    c. advise, in accordance with Member State law, the national parliament, the government, and other institutions and bodies on legislative and administrative measures relating to the protection of natural persons' rights and freedoms with regard to processing;

    d. promote the awareness of controllers and processors of their obligations under this Regulation;

    e. upon request, provide information to any data subject concerning the exercise of their rights under this Regulation and, if appropriate, cooperate with the supervisory authorities in other Member States to that end;

    f. handle complaints lodged by a data subject, or by a body, organisation or association in accordance with Article 80, and investigate, to the extent appropriate, the subject matter of the complaint and inform the complainant of the progress and the outcome of the investigation within a reasonable period, in particular if further investigation or coordination with another supervisory authority is necessary;

6

g. cooperate with, including sharing information and provide mutual assistance to, other supervisory authorities with a view to ensuring the consistency of application and enforcement of this Regulation;

h. conduct investigations on the application of this Regulation, including on the basis of information received from another supervisory authority or other public authority;

i. monitor relevant developments, insofar as they have an impact on the protection of personal data, in particular the development of information and communication technologies and commercial practices;

j. adopt standard contractual clauses referred to in Article 28(8) and in point (d) of Article 46(2);

k. establish and maintain a list in relation to the requirement for data protection impact assessment pursuant to Article 35(4);

l. give advice on the processing operations referred to in Article 36(2);

m. encourage the drawing up of codes of conduct pursuant to Article 40(1) and provide an opinion and approve such codes of conduct which provide sufficient safeguards, pursuant to Article 40(5);

n. encourage the establishment of data protection certification mechanisms and of data protection seals and marks pursuant to Article 42(1), and approve the criteria of certification pursuant to Article 42(5);

o. where applicable, carry out a periodic review of certifications issued in accordance with Article 42(7);

p. draft and publish the criteria for accreditation of a body for monitoring codes of conduct pursuant to Article 41 and of a certification body pursuant to Article 43;

q. conduct the accreditation of a body for monitoring codes of conduct pursuant to Article 41 and of a certification body pursuant to Article 43;

r. authorise contractual clauses and provisions referred to in Article 46(3);

s. approve binding corporate rules pursuant to Article 47;

t. contribute to the activities of the Board;

u. keep internal records of infringements of this Regulation and of measures taken in accordance with Article 58(2); and

v. fulfil any other tasks related to the protection of personal data.

2. Each supervisory authority shall facilitate the submission of complaints referred to in point (f) of paragraph 1 by measures such as a complaint submission form which can also be completed electronically, without excluding other means of communication.

3. The performance of the tasks of each supervisory authority shall be free of charge for the data subject and, where applicable, for the data protection officer.

4. Where requests are manifestly unfounded or excessive, in particular because of their repetitive character, the supervisory authority may charge a reasonable fee based on administrative costs, or refuse to act on the request. The supervisory authority shall bear the burden of demonstrating the manifestly unfounded or excessive character of the request.

6

Easy Peasy Summary

- Supervisory authorities are responsible for:

  o monitoring and enforcing the application of this Regulation;

  o promoting public awareness and understanding;

  o advising on legislative and administrative measures related to protecting rights and freedoms;

  o informing controllers/processors of their obligations;

  o handling complaints from data subjects;

  o investigating the subject matter of the complaint;

  o keeping the data subject informed of the progress and the outcome timely;

  o cooperating with other supervisory authorities;

  o conducting investigations based on information received from other supervisory authorities or public authorities;

  o monitoring relevant developments that have an impact on personal data protection;

  o adopting standard contractual clauses;

  o maintaining a list for data protection impact assessment requirements;

  o giving advice on certain processing operations;

  o encouraging codes of conduct;

  o establishing data protection certification mechanisms and seals/marks;

Supervisory authorities are responsible for ... encouraging codes of conduct ...

- ○ carrying out periodic reviews of certifications (if applicable);

- ○ drafting/publishing requirements for accreditation of bodies for monitoring codes of conduct or certification bodies;

- ○ authorising contractual clauses/provisions;

- ○ approving Binding Corporate Rules;

- ○ contributing to activities of the Board;

- ○ keeping internal records of infringements and measures taken; and

- ○ as well as any other tasks related to protecting personal data.

- Each supervisory authority should have a process in place for complaints to be submitted electronically or otherwise.

- Supervisory authorities are free of charge for data subjects and data protection officers.

- The supervisory authority can refuse to act or charge a fee where the request is manifestly unfounded or excessive. The burden is on the supervisory authority to prove the request really is manifestly unfounded or excessive.

The supervisory authority can refuse to act or charge a fee ...

6

Article 58

Powers

Official GDPR Text

1. Each supervisory authority shall have all of the following investigative powers:

   a. to order the controller and the processor, and, where applicable, the controller's or the processor's representative, to provide any information it requires for the performance of its tasks;

   b. to carry out investigations in the form of data protection audits;

   c. to carry out a review on certifications issued pursuant to Article 42(7);

   d. to notify the controller or the processor of an alleged infringement of this Regulation;

   e. to obtain, from the controller and the processor, access to all personal data and to all information necessary for the performance of its tasks;

   f. to obtain access to any premises of the controller and the processor, including to any data processing equipment and means, in accordance with Union or Member State procedural law.

2. Each supervisory authority shall have all of the following corrective powers:

   a. to issue warnings to a controller or processor that intended processing operations are likely to infringe provisions of this Regulation;

b. to issue reprimands to a controller or a processor where processing operations have infringed provisions of this Regulation;

c. to order the controller or the processor to comply with the data subject's requests to exercise his or her rights pursuant to this Regulation;

d. to order the controller or processor to bring processing operations into compliance with the provisions of this Regulation, where appropriate, in a specified manner and within a specified period;

e. to order the controller to communicate a personal data breach to the data subject;

f. to impose a temporary or definitive limitation including a ban on processing;

g. to order the rectification or erasure of personal data or restriction of processing pursuant to Articles 16, 17 and 18 and the notification of such actions to recipients to whom the personal data have been disclosed pursuant to Article 17(2) and Article 19;

h. to withdraw a certification or to order the certification body to withdraw a certification issued pursuant to Articles 42 and 43, or to order the certification body not to issue certification if the requirements for the certification are not or are no longer met;

i. to impose an administrative fine pursuant to Article 83, in addition to, or instead of measures referred to in this paragraph, depending on the circumstances of each individual case;

j. to order the suspension of data flows to a recipient in a third country or to an international organisation.

6

3. Each supervisory authority shall have all of the following authorisation and advisory powers:

   a. to advise the controller in accordance with the prior consultation procedure referred to in Article 36;

   b. to issue, on its own initiative or on request, opinions to the national parliament, the Member State government or, in accordance with Member State law, to other institutions and bodies as well as to the public on any issue related to the protection of personal data;

   c. to authorise processing referred to in Article 36(5), if the law of the Member State requires such prior authorisation;

   d. to issue an opinion and approve draft codes of conduct pursuant to Article 40(5);

   e. to accredit certification bodies pursuant to Article 43;

   f. to issue certifications and approve criteria of certification in accordance with Article 42(5);

   g. to adopt standard data protection clauses referred to in Article 28(8) and in point (d) of Article 46(2);

   h. to authorise contractual clauses referred to in point (a) of Article 46(3);

   i. to authorise administrative arrangements referred to in point (b) of Article 46(3);

   j. to approve binding corporate rules pursuant to Article 47.

4. The exercise of the powers conferred on the supervisory authority pursuant to this Article shall be subject to appropriate safeguards, including effective judicial remedy and due process, set out in Union and Member State law in accordance with the Charter.

5. Each Member State shall provide by law that its supervisory authority shall have the power to bring infringements of this Regulation to the attention of the judicial authorities and where appropriate, to commence or engage otherwise in legal proceedings, in order to enforce the provisions of this Regulation.

6. Each Member State may provide by law that its supervisory authority shall have additional powers to those referred to in paragraphs 1, 2 and 3. The exercise of those powers shall not impair the effective operation of Chapter VII.

Easy Peasy Summary

- A supervisory authority has investigative powers to:

    o order a controller, a processor, and/or their representative to provide any information required;

    o carry out data protection audits;

    o review certifications;

    o notify the controller or processor of an alleged violation of this Regulation;

    o obtain access all to personal data and information from the controller or processor;

    o get access to premises, including any data processing equipment.

- A supervisory authority has corrective powers to:

    o issue warnings

    o reprimand a controller or processor;

A supervisory authority has investigative powers to ... carry out data protection audits ...

6

- order the controller or processor to comply with the data subject's requests;

- order the controller or processor to bring processing operations into compliance within a given time;

- order the controller to inform data subjects of a personal data breach;

- impose temporary or definitive limitations or bans on processing;

- order personal data to be rectified, erased or restricted from processing;

- withdraw certification or forbid certification if requirements are not met;

- impose a fine instead of, or in addition to, other measures;

- order suspension of data flows to third countries or international organisations.

- The supervisory authority has advisory powers to:

  - advise the controller;

  - issue opinions to national parliament, Member State government or other public institutions on data protection issues;

  - authorise processing (if required by Member State law);

  - issue opinion and approve draft codes of conduct;

  - accredit certification bodies;

  - issue certifications and approve criteria of certification;

  - adopt standard data protection clauses;

  - authorise contractual clauses;

The supervisory authority has advisory powers to ... authorise contractual clauses ...

- authorise administrative arrangements;

- approve Binding Corporate Rules.

• Supervisory authorities must use safeguards that follow the laws of the Union and Member States to exercise their powers in an appropriate way.

• Each Member State should provide legal powers for its supervisory authority to bring infringements of this Regulation to the attention of judicial authorities, and if necessary, take legal action to enforce it.

A Member State may provide additional powers.

• A Member State may provide additional powers.

6

Article 59

Activity Reports

Official GDPR Text

Each supervisory authority shall draw up an annual report on its activities, which may include a list of types of infringement notified and types of measures taken in accordance with Article 58(2). Those reports shall be transmitted to the national parliament, the government and other authorities as designated by Member State law. They shall be made available to the public, to the Commission and to the Board.

Easy Peasy Summary

The reports must be made public and also sent to the Commission and Board.

- Supervisory authorities have to create an annual report on their activities and share it with the national parliament, the government, and so on.

- This report should include a list summarizing the infringements they were notified of and the measures they took.

- The reports must be made public and also sent to the Commission and Board.

7

Cooperation and Consistency

Article 60

Cooperation Between the Lead Supervisory Authority and the Other Supervisory Authorities Concerned

Official GDPR Text

1. The lead supervisory authority shall cooperate with the other supervisory authorities concerned in accordance with this Article in an endeavour to reach consensus. The lead supervisory authority and the supervisory authorities concerned shall exchange all relevant information with each other.

2. The lead supervisory authority may request at any time other supervisory authorities concerned to provide mutual assistance pursuant to Article 61 and may conduct joint operations pursuant to Article 62, in particular for carrying out investigations or for monitoring the implementation of a measure concerning a controller or processor established in another Member State.

3. The lead supervisory authority shall, without delay, communicate the relevant information on the matter to the other supervisory authorities concerned. It shall without delay submit a draft decision to the other supervisory authorities concerned for their opinion and take due account of their views.

4. Where any of the other supervisory authorities concerned within a period of four weeks after having been consulted in accordance with paragraph 3 of this Article, expresses a relevant and reasoned objection to the draft decision, the lead supervisory authority shall, if it does not follow the relevant and reasoned objection or is of the opinion that the objection is not relevant or reasoned, submit the matter to the consistency mechanism referred to in Article 63.

5. Where the lead supervisory authority intends to follow the relevant and reasoned objection made, it shall submit to the other supervisory authorities concerned a revised draft decision for their opinion. That revised draft decision shall be subject to the procedure referred to in paragraph 4 within a period of two weeks.

6. Where none of the other supervisory authorities concerned has objected to the draft decision submitted by the lead supervisory authority within the period referred to in paragraphs 4 and 5, the lead supervisory authority and the supervisory authorities concerned shall be deemed to be in agreement with that draft decision and shall be bound by it.

7. The lead supervisory authority shall adopt and notify the decision to the main establishment or single establishment of the controller or processor, as the case may be and inform the other supervisory authorities concerned and the Board of the decision in question, including a summary of the relevant facts and grounds. The supervisory authority with which a complaint has been lodged shall inform the complainant on the decision.

7

8. By derogation from paragraph 7, where a complaint is dismissed or rejected, the supervisory authority with which the complaint was lodged shall adopt the decision and notify it to the complainant and shall inform the controller thereof.

9. Where the lead supervisory authority and the supervisory authorities concerned agree to dismiss or reject parts of a complaint and to act on other parts of that complaint, a separate decision shall be adopted for each of those parts of the matter. The lead supervisory authority shall adopt the decision for the part concerning actions in relation to the controller, shall notify it to the main establishment or single establishment of the controller or processor on the territory of its Member State and shall inform the complainant thereof,

while the supervisory authority of the complainant shall adopt the decision for the part concerning dismissal or rejection of that complaint, and shall notify it to that complainant and shall inform the controller or processor thereof.

10. After being notified of the decision of the lead supervisory authority pursuant to paragraphs 7 and 9, the controller or processor shall take the necessary measures to ensure compliance with the decision as regards processing activities in the context of all its establishments in the Union. The controller or processor shall notify the measures taken for complying with the decision to the lead supervisory authority, which shall inform the other supervisory authorities concerned.

11. Where, in exceptional circumstances, a supervisory authority concerned has reasons to consider that there is an urgent need to act in order to protect the interests of data subjects, the urgency procedure referred to in Article 66 shall apply.

12. The lead supervisory authority and the other supervisory authorities concerned shall supply the information required under this Article to each other by electronic means, using a standardised format.

Easy Peasy Summary

They should share all relevant information.

- The lead supervisory authority must cooperate with other supervisory authorities to reach an agreement.

- They should share all relevant information.

- All communications and information shared between the lead supervisory authority and other supervisory authorities must be done electronically (in a standard format).

- The lead supervisory authority can request mutual assistance and conduct joint operations.

- The lead supervisory authority must also communicate all relevant information with the other supervisory authorities.

- The lead supervisory authority should submit a draft decision for their opinion and take their views into account.

- The lead supervisory authority must submit the matter to the consistency mechanism if any of the other supervisory authorities have raised (relevant and reasoned) objections within 4 weeks of to the draft decision.

- Where the lead supervisory authority decides to act on the objections, they should submit a revised draft decision and wait 2 weeks for the other supervisory authorities to share their opinion on the revised draft decision.

- If there are no objections within these 2 weeks, it is assumed they are in agreement.

- The lead supervisory authority should adopt the decision and notify the controller/processor. They should also inform other supervisory authorities and the Board.

- If a supervisory authority dismisses or rejects a complaint (that was lodged with them), they must notify the complainant of their decision and inform the controller.

- If only parts of a complaint are dismissed or rejected, separate decisions shall be adopted for each complaint point.

- The supervisory authority with which the complaint was lodged will handle the dismissal or rejection of those parts of the complaint.

The lead supervisory authority can ... conduct joint operations.

7

- The lead supervisory authority will deal with the rest of the complaint against the controller. The lead supervisory authority will notify the controller and the complainant of their decision.

- The controller or processor must take steps to achieve compliance once they have been notified of a decision.

- They must inform the lead supervisory authority of the measures they have taken to ensure compliance. The lead supervisory authority will then inform the other supervisory authorities.

An urgency procedure may be used to protect data subjects ...

- An urgency procedure may be used to protect data subjects in exceptional circumstances.

Article 61

Mutual Assistance

Official GDPR Text

1. Supervisory authorities shall provide each other with relevant information and mutual assistance in order to implement and apply this Regulation in a consistent manner, and shall put in place measures for effective cooperation with one another. Mutual assistance shall cover, in particular, information requests and supervisory measures, such as requests to carry out prior authorisations and consultations, inspections and investigations.

2. Each supervisory authority shall take all appropriate measures required to reply to a request of another supervisory authority without undue delay and no later than one month after receiving the request. Such measures may include, in particular, the transmission of relevant information on the conduct of an investigation.

3. Requests for assistance shall contain all the necessary information, including the purpose of and reasons for the request. Information exchanged shall be used only for the purpose for which it was requested.

4. The requested supervisory authority shall not refuse to comply with the request unless:

   a. it is not competent for the subject-matter of the request or for the measures it is requested to execute; or

   b. compliance with the request would infringe this Regulation or Union or Member State law to which the supervisory authority receiving the request is subject.

7

5. The requested supervisory authority shall inform the requesting supervisory authorities of the results or, as the case may be, of the progress of the measures taken in order to respond to the request. The requested supervisory authority shall provide reasons for any refusal to comply with a request pursuant to paragraph 4.

6. Requested supervisory authorities shall, as a rule, supply the information requested by other supervisory authorities by electronic means, using a standardised format.

7. Requested supervisory authorities shall not charge a fee for any action taken by them pursuant to a request for mutual assistance. Supervisory authorities may agree on rules to indemnify each other for specific expenditure arising from the provision of mutual assistance in exceptional circumstances.

8. Where a supervisory authority does not provide the information referred to in paragraph 5 of this Article within one month of receiving the request of another supervisory authority, the requesting supervisory authority may adopt a provisional measure on the territory of its Member State in accordance with Article 55(1). In that case, the urgent need to act under Article 66(1) shall be presumed to be met and require an urgent binding decision from the Board pursuant to Article 66(2).

9. The Commission may, by means of implementing acts, specify the format and procedures for mutual assistance referred to in this Article and the arrangements for the exchange of information by electronic means between supervisory authorities, and between supervisory authorities and the Board, in particular the standardised format referred to in paragraph 6 of this Article. Those implementing acts shall be adopted in accordance with the examination procedure referred to in Article 93(2).

Easy Peasy Summary

- Supervisory authorities must share information and assist each other to ensure this Regulation is applied consistently. This is known as mutual assistance. This includes requests for prior authorisations, consultations, inspections, and investigations.

- Requests for assistance should include all the relevant information. The request must include the purpose and reasons for the request. This information cannot be used for any other purpose.

- Everything possible should be done to ensure such a request is replied to within 1 month.

- Where appropriate, the supervisory authority receiving the request should also provide updates on the steps taken to comply with the order.

- A supervisory authority should not comply with a request if:

  o it is not competent to deal with the subject-matter of the request; or

  o if complying with the request would violate this Regulation; or

  o if complying with the request would violate Union or Member State law.

- If a request is refused, the supervisory authority that made the request should be informed of the reasons for the refusal.

- If a supervisory authority does not respond within a month, the requesting authority can take temporary action. This situation is considered urgent and needs a fast, binding decision from the Board

- Supervisory authorities cannot charge any fees for complying with a request for mutual assistance.

Everything possible should be done to ensure such a request is replied to within 1 month.

7

Article 62

Joint Operations of Supervisory Authorities

Official GDPR Text

1. The supervisory authorities shall, where appropriate, conduct joint operations including joint investigations and joint enforcement measures in which members or staff of the supervisory authorities of other Member States are involved.

2. Where the controller or processor has establishments in several Member States or where a significant number of data subjects in more than one Member State are likely to be substantially affected by processing operations, a supervisory authority of each of those Member States shall have the right to participate in joint operations. The supervisory authority which is competent pursuant to Article 56(1) or (4) shall invite the supervisory authority of each of those Member States to take part in the joint operations and shall respond without delay to the request of a supervisory authority to participate.

3. A supervisory authority may, in accordance with Member State law, and with the seconding supervisory authority's authorisation, confer powers, including investigative powers on the seconding supervisory authority's members or staff involved in joint operations or, in so far as the law of the Member State of the host supervisory authority permits, allow the seconding supervisory authority's members or staff to exercise their investigative powers in accordance with the law of the Member State of the seconding supervisory authority. Such investigative powers may be exercised only under the guidance and in the presence of members or staff of the host supervisory authority. The seconding supervisory authority's members or staff shall be subject to the Member State law of the host supervisory authority.

4. Where, in accordance with paragraph 1, staff of a seconding supervisory authority operate in another Member State, the Member State of the host supervisory authority shall assume responsibility for their actions, including liability, for any damage caused by them during their operations, in accordance with the law of the Member State in whose territory they are operating.

5. The Member State in whose territory the damage was caused shall make good such damage under the conditions applicable to damage caused by its own staff. The Member State of the seconding supervisory authority whose staff has caused damage to any person in the territory of another Member State shall reimburse that other Member State in full any sums it has paid to the persons entitled on their behalf.

6. Without prejudice to the exercise of its rights vis-à-vis third parties and with the exception of paragraph 5, each Member State shall refrain, in the case provided for in paragraph 1, from requesting reimbursement from another Member State in relation to damage referred to in paragraph 4.

7. Where a joint operation is intended and a supervisory authority does not, within one month, comply with the obligation laid down in the second sentence of paragraph 2 of this Article, the other supervisory authorities may adopt a provisional measure on the territory of its Member State in accordance with Article 55. In that case, the urgent need to act under Article 66(1) shall be presumed to be met and require an opinion or an urgent binding decision from the Board pursuant to Article 66(2).

7

Easy Peasy Summary

- Supervisory authorities can conduct joint operations, investigations and enforcement measures with members or staff of other Member States' supervisory authorities.

- If a controller or processor has branches in multiple Member States or processes personal data of data subjects across different Member States, each relevant supervisory authority can take part in joint operations.

- The competent supervisory authority should invite other relevant authorities (called seconding supervisory authorities) to take part.

... should respond quickly to requests from other supervisory authorities to participate.

- They should respond quickly to requests from other supervisory authorities to participate.

- A supervisory authority can give investigative powers to members or staff of the seconding supervisory authority during joint operations (as far as the host Member States allows).

- This can include allowing them to exercise their investigative powers in the seconding supervisory authority's Member State.

- These powers must only be used under the guidance and supervision the host supervisory authority (the seconding supervisory authority must comply with the laws of the host Member State).

- If staff from a seconding supervisory authority work in another Member State, the host supervisory authority's Member State will be responsible for their actions and liable for any damage they cause during their operations (in accordance with the laws of the host Member State where they are operating).

- If damage is caused by staff of a seconding supervisory authority in another Member State, the host Member State is responsible for compensating the affected parties (just as they would for their own staff's actions).

- The Member State of the seconding supervisory authority must reimburse the host Member State for payments made to the affected parties.

- Where joint operations, investigations and enforcement measures take place, a Member State cannot request reimbursement from another Member State (with the exception of paragraph 5 of this Article). However, they can still exercise their rights against third parties.

7

Article 63
Consistency Mechanism

Official GDPR Text

In order to contribute to the consistent application of this Regulation throughout the Union, the supervisory authorities shall cooperate with each other and, where relevant, with the Commission, through the consistency mechanism as set out in this Section.

Easy Peasy Summary

... collaborate with the Commission as necessary,

- The supervisory authorities must work together to make sure the Regulation is being applied consistently throughout the Union, using the consistency mechanism.

- They should also collaborate with the Commission as necessary.

Article 64

Opinion of the Board

Official GDPR Text

1. The Board shall issue an opinion where a competent supervisory authority intends to adopt any of the measures below. To that end, the competent supervisory authority shall communicate the draft decision to the Board, when it:

    a. aims to adopt a list of the processing operations subject to the requirement for a data protection impact assessment pursuant to Article 35(4);

    b. concerns a matter pursuant to Article 40(7) whether a draft code of conduct or an amendment or extension to a code of conduct complies with this Regulation;

    c. aims to approve the criteria for accreditation of a body pursuant to Article 41(3) or a certification body pursuant to Article 43(3);

    d. aims to determine standard data protection clauses referred to in point (d) of Article 46(2) and in Article 28(8);

    e. aims to authorise contractual clauses referred to in point (a) of Article 46(3); or

    f. aims to approve binding corporate rules within the meaning of Article 47.

2. Any supervisory authority, the Chair of the Board or the Commission may request that any matter of general application or producing effects in more than one Member State be examined by the Board with a view to obtaining an opinion, in particular where a competent supervisory authority does not comply with the obligations for mutual assistance in accordance with Article 61 or for joint operations in accordance with Article 62.

7

3. In the cases referred to in paragraphs 1 and 2, the Board shall issue an opinion on the matter submitted to it provided that it has not already issued an opinion on the same matter. That opinion shall be adopted within eight weeks by simple majority of the members of the Board. That period may be extended by a further six weeks, taking into account the complexity of the subject matter. Regarding the draft decision referred to in paragraph 1 circulated to the members of the Board in accordance with paragraph 5, a member which has not objected within a reasonable period indicated by the Chair, shall be deemed to be in agreement with the draft decision.

4. Supervisory authorities and the Commission shall, without undue delay, communicate by electronic means to the Board, using a standardised format any relevant information, including as the case may be a summary of the facts, the draft decision, the grounds which make the enactment of such measure necessary, and the views of other supervisory authorities concerned.

5. The Chair of the Board shall, without undue, delay inform by electronic means:

    a. the members of the Board and the Commission of any relevant information which has been communicated to it using a standardised format. The secretariat of the Board shall, where necessary, provide translations of relevant information; and

    b. the supervisory authority referred to, as the case may be, in paragraphs 1 and 2, and the Commission of the opinion and make it public.

6. The competent supervisory authority shall not adopt its draft decision referred to in paragraph 1 within the period referred to in paragraph 3.

7. The supervisory authority referred to in paragraph 1 shall take utmost account of the opinion of the Board and shall, within two weeks after receiving the opinion, communicate to the Chair of the Board by electronic means whether it will maintain or amend its draft decision and, if any, the amended draft decision, using a standardised format.

8. Where the supervisory authority concerned informs the Chair of the Board within the period referred to in paragraph 7 of this Article that it does not intend to follow the opinion of the Board, in whole or in part, providing the relevant grounds, Article 65(1) shall apply.

Easy Peasy Summary

- The Board will issue an opinion when a competent supervisory authority intends to adopt any of the following measures:

  ○ creating a list of processing operations that require a data protection impact assessment;

  ○ determining whether a draft code of conduct, amendment or extension is compliant;

  ○ deciding the criteria for accreditation or certification of a body;

  ○ determining standard data protection clauses;

  ○ authorising ad hoc contractual clauses; or

  ○ approving Binding Corporate Rules.

- Any supervisory authority, the Chair of the Board, or the Commission can ask the Board for an opinion on any matter that affects more than one Member State.

7

- This could also be when a competent supervisory authority does not comply with its mutual assistance or joint operations obligations.

- When a supervisory authority does not comply with its mutual assistance or joint operations obligations, any supervisory authority, the Chair of the Board or the Commission can make a request to the Board to have a look and provide an opinion. The Board will issue an opinion (as long as it has not already done so).

The opinion should be adopted within 8 weeks ... by a simple majority.

- This opinion should be adopted within 8 weeks (14 weeks for more complex matters) by a simple majority.

- The supervisory authority should wait until this period is over prior to adopting the draft decision.

- Unless a board member objects, draft decisions that have been circulated to Board members will be assumed to have been accepted.

- Supervisory authorities and the Commission must communicate electronically with the Board.

- Relevant information such as a summary of the facts, the draft decision, the grounds for enacting the measure, and any views of other supervisory authorities should be included.

- The supervisory authority must consider the opinion and confirm whether it will maintain or amend its draft decision and let the board know within 2 weeks.

- The Dispute Resolution mechanism will apply, if the supervisory authority does not accept (either wholly or partially) the opinion of the Board.

Article 65

Dispute Resolution by the Board

Official GDPR Text

1. In order to ensure the correct and consistent application of this Regulation in individual cases, the Board shall adopt a binding decision in the following cases:

   a. where, in a case referred to in Article 60(4), a supervisory authority concerned has raised a relevant and reasoned objection to a draft decision of the lead authority or the lead authority has rejected such an objection as being not relevant or reasoned. The binding decision shall concern all the matters which are the subject of the relevant and reasoned objection, in particular whether there is an infringement of this Regulation;

   b. where there are conflicting views on which of the supervisory authorities concerned is competent for the main establishment;

   c. where a competent supervisory authority does not request the opinion of the Board in the cases referred to in Article 64(1), or does not follow the opinion of the Board issued under Article 64. In that case, any supervisory authority concerned or the Commission may communicate the matter to the Board.

2. The decision referred to in paragraph 1 shall be adopted within one month from the referral of the subject-matter by a two-thirds majority of the members of the Board. That period may be extended by a further month on account of the complexity of the subject-matter. The decision referred to in paragraph 1 shall be reasoned and addressed to the lead supervisory authority and all the supervisory authorities concerned and binding on them.

7

3. Where the Board has been unable to adopt a decision within the periods referred to in paragraph 2, it shall adopt its decision within two weeks following the expiration of the second month referred to in paragraph 2 by a simple majority of the members of the Board. Where the members of the Board are split, the decision shall by adopted by the vote of its Chair.

4. The supervisory authorities concerned shall not adopt a decision on the subject matter submitted to the Board under paragraph 1 during the periods referred to in paragraphs 2 and 3.

5. The Chair of the Board shall notify, without undue delay, the decision referred to in paragraph 1 to the supervisory authorities concerned. It shall inform the Commission thereof. The decision shall be published on the website of the Board without delay after the supervisory authority has notified the final decision referred to in paragraph 6.

6. The lead supervisory authority or, as the case may be, the supervisory authority with which the complaint has been lodged, shall adopt its final decision on the basis of the decision referred to in paragraph 1 of this Article, without undue delay and at the latest by one month after the Board has notified its decision. The lead supervisory authority or, as the case may be, the supervisory authority with which the complaint has been lodged, shall inform the Board of the date when its final decision is notified respectively to the controller or the processor and to the data subject. The final decision of the supervisory authorities concerned shall be adopted under the terms of Article 60(7), (8) and (9). The final decision shall refer to the decision referred to in paragraph 1 of this Article and shall specify that the decision referred to in that paragraph will be published on the website of the Board in accordance with paragraph 5 of this Article. The final decision shall attach the decision referred to in paragraph 1 of this Article.

Easy Peasy Summary

- To make sure the Regulation is applied correctly and consistently, the Board will make binding decision in these cases:

  - where a concerned supervisory authority has raised an objection and the lead supervisory authority has rejected it as irrelevant;

  - where there are conflicting views on which supervisory authority is the competent supervisory authority;

  - where the supervisory authority does not request or follow the opinion of the Board as per Article 64.

- A complaint against such a supervisory authority can be made by other supervisory authorities or the Commission.

- The decision must be:

  - adopted within one month (2 months for complex matters);

  - reasoned, addressed to the lead supervisory authority and all the supervisory authorities concerned and will be binding; and

  - made by a two-thirds majority of the members of the Board.

- If the Board is unable to make a decision within 2 months, it must do so within the next 2 weeks by a simple majority. If members are split, the Chair will have the deciding vote.

- The binding decision shall be published on the Board's website.

7

The binding decision shall be published on the Board's website.

- The lead supervisory authority (or the supervisory authority to whom the complaints were made) will:

  o adopt its final decision based on the Board's decision, latest within 1 month from its notification; and

  o notify the Board once the final decision is communicated to the controller or processor and to the data subject.

The final decision should mention and attach the binding decision of the Board ...

- The final decision should mention and attach the binding decision of the Board and specify that the decision will be published on the Board's website.

Article 66

Urgency Procedure

Official GDPR Text

1. In exceptional circumstances, where a supervisory authority concerned considers that there is an urgent need to act in order to protect the rights and freedoms of data subjects, it may, by way of derogation from the consistency mechanism referred to in Articles 63, 64 and 65 or the procedure referred to in Article 60, immediately adopt provisional measures intended to produce legal effects on its own territory with a specified period of validity which shall not exceed three months. The supervisory authority shall, without delay, communicate those measures and the reasons for adopting them to the other supervisory authorities concerned, to the Board and to the Commission.

2. Where a supervisory authority has taken a measure pursuant to paragraph 1 and considers that final measures need urgently be adopted, it may request an urgent opinion or an urgent binding decision from the Board, giving reasons for requesting such opinion or decision.

3. Any supervisory authority may request an urgent opinion or an urgent binding decision, as the case may be, from the Board where a competent supervisory authority has not taken an appropriate measure in a situation where there is an urgent need to act, in order to protect the rights and freedoms of data subjects, giving reasons for requesting such opinion or decision, including for the urgent need to act.

4. By derogation from Article 64(3) and Article 65(2), an urgent opinion or an urgent binding decision referred to in paragraphs 2 and 3 of this Article shall be adopted within two weeks by simple majority of the members of the Board.

7

Easy Peasy Summary

- Supervisory authorities may adopt provisional measures with legal effects to protect data subjects' rights in exceptional circumstances.

- These measures must be communicated to other supervisory authorities, the Board and the Commission, and their validity is limited to 3 months.

... may request an urgent opinion or binding decision from the Board to take final ... decisions.

- If a supervisory authority has taken provisional measures, they may request an urgent opinion or binding decision from the Board to take final and more permanent measures.

- Any supervisory authority may request an urgent opinion or decision from the Board, when a competent supervisory authority has not taken necessary action in an urgent situation that requires action to protect data subjects' rights.

- An urgent opinion or binding decision must be adopted within 2 weeks (by majority members of the Board).

Article 67

Exchange of Information

Official GDPR Text

The Commission may adopt implementing acts of general scope in order to specify the arrangements for the exchange of information by electronic means between supervisory authorities, and between supervisory authorities and the Board, in particular the standardised format referred to in Article 64.

Those implementing acts shall be adopted in accordance with the examination procedure referred to in Article 93(2).

Easy Peasy Summary

- The Commission can create general rules for communicating information electronically between supervisory authorities and the Board.

- This includes a standardised format for exchanging information.

7

Article 68

European Data Protection Board

Official GDPR Text

1. The European Data Protection Board (the 'Board') is hereby established as a body of the Union and shall have legal personality.

2. The Board shall be represented by its Chair.

3. The Board shall be composed of the head of one supervisory authority of each Member State and of the European Data Protection Supervisor, or their respective representatives.

4. Where in a Member State more than one supervisory authority is responsible for monitoring the application of the provisions pursuant to this Regulation, a joint representative shall be appointed in accordance with that Member State's law.

5. The Commission shall have the right to participate in the activities and meetings of the Board without voting right. The Commission shall designate a representative. The Chair of the Board shall communicate to the Commission the activities of the Board.

6. In the cases referred to in Article 65, the European Data Protection Supervisor shall have voting rights only on decisions which concern principles and rules applicable to the Union institutions, bodies, offices and agencies which correspond in substance to those of this Regulation.

Easy Peasy Summary

The European Data Protection (EDPB) is referred to as 'the Board'.

- The European Data Protection Board (EDPB) is referred to as 'the Board'.

- The Board is established as a body of the Union with legal personality.

- The Board is made up of:

  o a Chair who represents the Board;

  o the head of one supervisory authority of each Member State (or their representatives);

  o the head of the European Data Protection Supervisor (or its representative);

  o the Commission's representative.

- Where there is more than one supervisory authority in a Member State, a joint representative must be appointed to sit on the Board.

- The Commission's representative has no voting rights but can take part in meetings and other activities.

- The Chair will keep the Commission informed of the Board's activities.

- The European Data Protection Supervisor can only vote on decisions concerning principles and rules that apply to Union institutions, bodies, offices and agencies.

7

Article 69

Independence

Official GDPR Text

1. The Board shall act independently when performing its tasks or exercising its powers pursuant to Articles 70 and 71.

2. Without prejudice to requests by the Commission referred to in point (b) of Article 70(1) and in Article 70(2), the Board shall, in the performance of its tasks or the exercise of its powers, neither seek nor take instructions from anybody.

Easy Peasy Summary

The Board will act independently when carrying out its tasks and exerting its powers.

- The Board will act independently when carrying out its tasks and exerting its powers.

- The Board should not take or seek instructions from any person, except for requests by the Commission.

Article 70

Tasks of the Board

Official GDPR Text

1. The Board shall ensure the consistent application of this Regulation. To that end, the Board shall, on its own initiative or, where relevant, at the request of the Commission, in particular:

   a. monitor and ensure the correct application of this Regulation in the cases provided for in Articles 64 and 65 without prejudice to the tasks of national supervisory authorities;

   b. advise the Commission on any issue related to the protection of personal data in the Union, including on any proposed amendment of this Regulation;

   c. advise the Commission on the format and procedures for the exchange of information between controllers, processors and supervisory authorities for binding corporate rules;

   d. issue guidelines, recommendations, and best practices on procedures for erasing links, copies or replications of personal data from publicly available communication services as referred to in Article 17(2);

   e. examine, on its own initiative, on request of one of its members or on request of the Commission, any question covering the application of this Regulation and issue guidelines, recommendations and best practices in order to encourage consistent application of this Regulation;

   f. issue guidelines, recommendations and best practices in accordance with point (e) of this paragraph for further specifying the criteria and conditions for decisions based on profiling pursuant to Article 22(2);

7

g. issue guidelines, recommendations and best practices in accordance with point (e) of this paragraph for establishing the personal data breaches and determining the undue delay referred to in Article 33(1) and (2) and for the particular circumstances in which a controller or a processor is required to notify the personal data breach;

h. issue guidelines, recommendations and best practices in accordance with point (e) of this paragraph as to the circumstances in which a personal data breach is likely to result in a high risk to the rights and freedoms of the natural persons referred to in Article 34(1);

i. issue guidelines, recommendations and best practices in accordance with point (e) of this paragraph for the purpose of further specifying the criteria and requirements for personal data transfers based on binding corporate rules adhered to by controllers and binding corporate rules adhered to by processors and on further necessary requirements to ensure the protection of personal data of the data subjects concerned referred to in Article 47;

j. issue guidelines, recommendations and best practices in accordance with point (e) of this paragraph for the purpose of further specifying the criteria and requirements for the personal data transfers on the basis of Article 49(1);

k. draw up guidelines for supervisory authorities concerning the application of measures referred to in Article 58(1), (2) and (3) and the setting of administrative fines pursuant to Article 83;

l. review the practical application of the guidelines, recommendations and best practices referred to in points (e) and (f);

m. issue guidelines, recommendations and best practices in accordance with point (e) of this paragraph for establishing common procedures for reporting by natural persons of infringements of this Regulation pursuant to Article 54(2);

n. encourage the drawing-up of codes of conduct and the establishment of data protection certification mechanisms and data protection seals and marks pursuant to Articles 40 and 42;

o. carry out the accreditation of certification bodies and its period review pursuant to Article 43 and maintain a public register of accredited bodies pursuant to Article 43(6) and of the accredited controllers or processors established in third countries pursuant to Article 42(7);

p. specify the requirements referred to in Article 43(3) with a view to the accreditation of certification bodies under Article 42;

q. provide the Commission with an opinion on the certification requirements referred to in Article 43(8);

r. provide the Commission with an opinion on the icons referred to in Article 12(7);

s. provide the Commission with an opinion for the assessment of the adequacy of the level of protection in a third country or international organisation, including for the assessment whether a third country, a territory or one or more specified sectors within that third country, or an international organisation no longer ensures an adequate level of protection. To that end, the Commission shall provide the Board with all necessary documentation, including correspondence with the government of the third country, with regard to that third country, territory or specified sector, or with the international organisation;

7

t. issue opinions on draft decisions of supervisory authorities pursuant to the consistency mechanism referred to in Article 64(1), on matters submitted pursuant to Article 64(2) and to issue binding decisions pursuant to Article 65, including in cases referred to in Article 66;

u. promote the cooperation and the effective bilateral and multilateral exchange of information and best practices between the supervisory authorities;

v. promote common training programmes and facilitate personnel exchanges between the supervisory authorities and, where appropriate, with the supervisory authorities of third countries or with international organisations;

w. promote the exchange of knowledge and documentation on data protection legislation and practice with data protection supervisory authorities worldwide;

x. issue opinions on codes of conduct drawn up at Union level pursuant to Article 40(9); and

y. maintain a publicly accessible electronic register of decisions taken by supervisory authorities and courts on issues handled in the consistency mechanism.

2. Where the Commission requests advice from the Board, it may indicate a time limit, taking into account the urgency of the matter.

3. The Board shall forward its opinions, guidelines, recommendations, and best practices to the Commission and to the committee referred to in Article 93 and make them public.

4. The Board shall, where appropriate, consult interested parties and give them the opportunity to comment within a reasonable period. The Board shall, without prejudice to Article 76, make the results of the consultation procedure publicly available.

Easy Peasy Summary

- The Board must:

  o monitor and ensure the correct application of this Regulation;

  o review practical application of the guidelines, recommendations and best practices;

  o advise the Commission on:

    - any issue related to protecting personal data;

    - format and procedures for how information is communicated between controllers, processors and supervisory authorities.

  o examine questions covering how the Regulation is applied;

  o issue guidelines, recommendations and best practices for:

    - decisions based on profiling;

    - establishing personal data breaches and determining undue delay;

    - circumstances when a personal data breach is likely to result in a high risk;

    - specifying criteria and requirements for transfers based on Binding Corporate Rules;

    - reporting infringements of this Regulation;

    - procedures for erasing links, copies or replications of personal data from publicly available communication services.

The Board must monitor and ensure the correct application of this Regulation ...

7

- o draw up guidelines and set administrative fines for supervisory authorities;

- o encourage codes of conduct, data protection certification mechanisms and seals/marks;

- o approve criteria of certification;

- o maintain a public register of accredited bodies;

- o approve requirements for accreditation of certification bodies;

- o provide opinion on certification requirements;

- o provide opinion on adequacy decision;

- o provide the Commission with an opinion on icons;

- o give the Commission opinions on the level of protection in a third country;

- o issue opinions on:

  - draft decisions of supervisory authorities under the consistency mechanism; and

  - codes of conduct.

... promote cooperation and effective exchange of information/ best practice ...

- o promote:

  - cooperation and effective exchange of information/ best practice;

  - common training programmes;

  - facilitate personnel exchanges between the supervisory authorities;

  - exchange knowledge on data protection laws and practice worldwide.

○ keep an online register of decisions taken by supervisory authorities and courts in the consistency mechanism;

○ forward opinions, guidelines, recommendations and best practices to the Commission and the Committee and make them public;

○ consult interested parties and offer them the opportunity to comment.

- The Commission can set a time limit for advice requested from the Board, depending on how urgent the matter is.

The Commission can set a time limit for advise requested from the Board ...

7

Article 71

Reports

Official GDPR Text

1. The Board shall draw up an annual report regarding the protection of natural persons with regard to processing in the Union and, where relevant, in third countries and international organisations. The report shall be made public and be transmitted to the European Parliament, to the Council and to the Commission.

2. The annual report shall include a review of the practical application of the guidelines, recommendations and best practices referred to in point (l) of Article 70(1) as well as of the binding decisions referred to in Article 65.

Easy Peasy Summary

The Board must produce an annual report.

- The Board must produce an annual report. The report must include:

    o   a review of practical application of guidelines;

    o   recommendations and best practices; and

    o   binding decisions.

- The report should be shared with:

    o   the EU Parliament;

    o   the Council;

    o   the Commission; and

    o   the public.

Article 72

Procedure

Official GDPR Text

1. The Board shall take decisions by a simple majority of its members, unless otherwise provided for in this Regulation.

2. The Board shall adopt its own rules of procedure by a two-thirds majority of its members and organise its own operational arrangements.

Easy Peasy Summary

• Decisions by the Board are made by a simple majority of its members, unless stated otherwise.

• The Board will create its own rules and operations with a two-thirds majority vote from its members.

Decisions by the Board are made by a simple majority of its members …

7

Article 73
Chair

Official GDPR Text

1. The Board shall elect a chair and two deputy chairs from amongst its members by simple majority.

2. The term of office of the Chair and of the deputy chairs shall be five years and be renewable once.

Easy Peasy Summary

Each term lasts for five years and can be renewed once.

- The Board must elect:

  ○ a Chair; and

  ○ two deputy Chairs from its members.

- Each term lasts for five years and can be renewed once.

Article 74

Tasks of the Chair

Official GDPR Text

1. The Chair shall have the following tasks:

    a. to convene the meetings of the Board and prepare its agenda;

    b. to notify decisions adopted by the Board pursuant to Article 65 to the lead supervisory authority and the supervisory authorities concerned;

    c. to ensure the timely performance of the tasks of the Board, in particular in relation to the consistency mechanism referred to in Article 63.

2. The Board shall lay down the allocation of tasks between the Chair and the deputy chairs in its rules of procedure.

7

Easy Peasy Summary

*   The Chair must:

    o   call meetings and prepare the agenda;

    o   notify decisions made by the Board to:

        *   the lead supervisory authority; and

        *   any concerned supervisory authorities.

    o   make sure tasks are completed in good time.

*   The Board will allocate tasks between the Chair and the deputy Chairs in its rules of procedure.

Article 75

Secretariat

Official GDPR Text

1. The Board shall have a secretariat, which shall be provided by the European Data Protection Supervisor.

2. The secretariat shall perform its tasks exclusively under the instructions of the Chair of the Board.

3. The staff of the European Data Protection Supervisor involved in carrying out the tasks conferred on the Board by this Regulation shall be subject to separate reporting lines from the staff involved in carrying out tasks conferred on the European Data Protection Supervisor.

4. Where appropriate, the Board and the European Data Protection Supervisor shall establish and publish a Memorandum of Understanding implementing this Article, determining the terms of their cooperation, and applicable to the staff of the European Data Protection Supervisor involved in carrying out the tasks conferred on the Board by this Regulation.

5. The secretariat shall provide analytical, administrative and logistical support to the Board.

6. The secretariat shall be responsible in particular for:

   a. the day-to-day business of the Board;

   b. communication between the members of the Board, its Chair and the Commission;

   c. communication with other institutions and the public;

   d. the use of electronic means for the internal and external communication;

   e. the translation of relevant information;

f.   the preparation and follow-up of the meetings of the Board;

g.   the preparation, drafting and publication of opinions, decisions on the settlement of disputes between supervisory authorities and other texts adopted by the Board.

Easy Peasy Summary

- The European Data Protection Supervisor will provide a Secretariat to the Board.

- The Secretariat will only take instructions from the Chair of the Board.

- The staff working on the Board's tasks must have a separate reporting line from those working on the European Data Protection Supervisor's tasks.

- The Board and European Data Protection Supervisor will create and share a Memorandum of Understanding that outlines how they will work together on tasks, specifically for the staff involved in the Board's tasks.

- The Secretariat will help the Board with analytical, administrative and logistical support.

- The Secretariat has various responsibilities including:

  o   managing the daily tasks of the Board;

  o   communication between members, institutions and the public;

  o   using electronic means for communication;

  o   translating information;

  o   preparing and following up meetings;

  o   drafting and publishing opinions and other texts.

The European Data Protection Supervisor will provide a Secretariat …

7

Article 76

Confidentiality

Official GDPR Text

1. The discussions of the Board shall be confidential where the Board deems it necessary, as provided for in its rules of procedure.

2. Access to documents submitted to members of the Board, experts and representatives of third parties shall be governed by Regulation (EC) No 1049/2001 of the European Parliament and of the Council.

Easy Peasy Summary

The Board can keep discussions confidential if needed ...

- The Board can keep discussions confidential if needed, following its rules of procedure.

- Access to documents given to Board members, experts and third-party representatives will follow Regulation (EC) No 1049/2001 of the European Parliament and Council.

8

Remedies, Liability and Penalties

Article 77

Right to Lodge a Complaint With a Supervisory Authority

Official GDPR Text

1. Without prejudice to any other administrative or judicial remedy, every data subject shall have the right to lodge a complaint with a supervisory authority, in particular in the Member State of his or her habitual residence, place of work or place of the alleged infringement if the data subject considers that the processing of personal data relating to him or her infringes this Regulation.

2. The supervisory authority with which the complaint has been lodged shall inform the complainant on the progress and the outcome of the complaint including the possibility of a judicial remedy pursuant to Article 78.

Easy Peasy Summary

... will not affect administrative or judicial remedies also available to them.

*   Every data subject has the right to lodge a complaint with a supervisory authority where they live, work or the place of infringement, if they believe the processing of their personal data violates this Regulation.

*   This will not affect administrative or judicial remedies also available to them.

*   The concerned supervisory authority will keep the data subject informed on:

    o   the progress;

    o   the outcome of the complaint; and

    o   their option to approach the court.

Article 78

Right to an Effective Judicial Remedy Against a Supervisory Authority

Official GDPR Text

1. Without prejudice to any other administrative or non-judicial remedy, each natural or legal person shall have the right to an effective judicial remedy against a legally binding decision of a supervisory authority concerning them.

2. Without prejudice to any other administrative or non-judicial remedy, each data subject shall have the right to an effective judicial remedy where the supervisory authority which is competent pursuant to Articles 55 and 56 does not handle a complaint or does not inform the data subject within three months on the progress or outcome of the complaint lodged pursuant to Article 77.

3. Proceedings against a supervisory authority shall be brought before the courts of the Member State where the supervisory authority is established.

4. Where proceedings are brought against a decision of a supervisory authority which was preceded by an opinion or a decision of the Board in the consistency mechanism, the supervisory authority shall forward that opinion or decision to the court.

8

Easy Peasy Summary

- Every person has the right to an effective judicial remedy against a legally binding decision of a supervisory authority.

- Data subjects have the right to a judicial remedy if the supervisory authority does not handle their complaint or inform them within 3 months on the status or conclusion of the complaint.

Proceedings against a supervisory authority must take placed in the Member State where it is located.

- This will not affect the administrative or non-judicial remedies also available to them.

- Proceedings against a supervisory authority must take place in the Member State where it is located.

- Where proceedings are based on the opinion or decision of the Board, the supervisory authority must forward the opinion or decision to the court.

Article 79

Right to an Effective Judicial Remedy Against a Controller or Processor

Official GDPR Text

1. Without prejudice to any available administrative or non-judicial remedy, including the right to lodge a complaint with a supervisory authority pursuant to Article 77, each data subject shall have the right to an effective judicial remedy where he or she considers that his or her rights under this Regulation have been infringed as a result of the processing of his or her personal data in non-compliance with this Regulation.

2. Proceedings against a controller or a processor shall be brought before the courts of the Member State where the controller or processor has an establishment. Alternatively, such proceedings may be brought before the courts of the Member State where the data subject has his or her habitual residence, unless the controller or processor is a public authority of a Member State acting in the exercise of its public powers.

Easy Peasy Summary

8

- Data subjects have the right to judicial remedy if their rights have been infringed as a result of non-compliance with this Regulation.

- This will not affect other administrative or non-judicial remedies, including complaining to a supervisory authority.

- The proceedings can take place either in the Member State the controller or processor is based, or where the data subject lives.

Article 80
Representation of Data Subjects

Official GDPR Text

1. The data subject shall have the right to mandate a not-for-profit body, organisation or association which has been properly constituted in accordance with the law of a Member State, has statutory objectives which are in the public interest, and is active in the field of the protection of data subjects' rights and freedoms with regard to the protection of their personal data to lodge the complaint on his or her behalf, to exercise the rights referred to in Articles 77, 78 and 79 on his or her behalf, and to exercise the right to receive compensation referred to in Article 82 on his or her behalf where provided for by Member State law.

2. Member States may provide that any body, organisation or association referred to in paragraph 1 of this Article, independently of a data subject's mandate, has the right to lodge, in that Member State, a complaint with the supervisory authority which is competent pursuant to Article 77 and to exercise the rights referred to in Articles 78 and 79 if it considers that the rights of a data subject under this Regulation have been infringed as a result of the processing.

Easy Peasy Summary

- Data subjects can appoint an organisation (not-for-profit body or association) to:

  o   make a complaint;

  o   exercise their rights; and

  o   receive compensation,

  on their behalf, provided the organisation focuses on data protection rights and has been set up as per Member State law.

- Any person, organisation or association (mentioned in paragraph 1) can:

  o   file a complaint with the competent supervisory authority if they believe that a data subject's rights have been violated; and

  o   exercise the rights mentioned in Articles 78 and 79, according to Member States' laws.

8

Article 81
Suspension of Proceedings

Official GDPR Text

1. Where a competent court of a Member State has information on proceedings, concerning the same subject matter as regards processing by the same controller or processor, that are pending in a court in another Member State, it shall contact that court in the other Member State to confirm the existence of such proceedings.

2. Where proceedings concerning the same subject matter as regards processing of the same controller or processor are pending in a court in another Member State, any competent court other than the court first seized may suspend its proceedings.

3. Where those proceedings are pending at first instance, any court other than the court first seized may also, on the application of one of the parties, decline jurisdiction if the court first seized has jurisdiction over the actions in question and its law permits the consolidation thereof.

Easy Peasy Summary

If any court ... is involved, it can suspend its proceedings.

- If a court in one Member State knows of proceedings involving the same controller or processor, and subject matter is also pending in another Member State, it should contact that court to confirm the existence of such proceedings.

- If any court (other than the original) is involved, it can suspend its proceedings.

- Any court other than the original can decline jurisdiction if the original court has jurisdiction and its law allows consolidation of proceedings.

Article 82

Right to Compensation and Liability

Official GDPR Text

1. Any person who has suffered material or non-material damage as a result of an infringement of this Regulation shall have the right to receive compensation from the controller or processor for the damage suffered.

2. Any controller involved in processing shall be liable for the damage caused by processing which infringes this Regulation. A processor shall be liable for the damage caused by processing only where it has not complied with obligations of this Regulation specifically directed to processors or where it has acted outside or contrary to lawful instructions of the controller.

3. A controller or processor shall be exempt from liability under paragraph 2 if it proves that it is not in any way responsible for the event giving rise to the damage.

4. Where more than one controller or processor, or both a controller and a processor, are involved in the same processing and where they are, under paragraphs 2 and 3, responsible for any damage caused by processing, each controller or processor shall be held liable for the entire damage in order to ensure effective compensation of the data subject.

5. Where a controller or processor has, in accordance with paragraph 4, paid full compensation for the damage suffered, that controller or processor shall be entitled to claim back from the other controllers or processors involved in the same processing that part of the compensation corresponding to their part of responsibility for the damage, in accordance with the conditions set out in paragraph 2.

8

6. Court proceedings for exercising the right to receive compensation shall be brought before the courts competent under the law of the Member State referred to in Article 79(2).

Easy Peasy Summary

Controllers are liable for any damage caused by processing that violates this Regulation.

- Data subjects have the right to receive compensation from the controller or processor if they suffer material or non-material damage.

- Controllers are liable for any damage caused by processing that violates this Regulation.

- Processors are only liable if:

    o they have failed to comply with Regulations directed at them; or

    o they acted outside of the written instructions of the controller.

- A controller or processor may be exempt from liability if they prove that they are not responsible for causing the damage.

- If more than one controller or processor (or both) are responsible for the same damage to the data subject, each of them will be held liable for the full amount of damage to ensure complete compensation for the individual.

- A controller or processor can reclaim the portion of responsibility for the damage from other controllers or processors involved, where they have already paid full compensation for the damage.

- Data subjects can take legal action to receive compensation in the courts of the relevant Member State.

Article 83

General Conditions for Imposing Administrative Fines

Official GDPR Text

1. Each supervisory authority shall ensure that the imposition of administrative fines pursuant to this Article in respect of infringements of this Regulation referred to in paragraphs 4, 5 and 6 shall in each individual case be effective, proportionate and dissuasive.

2. Administrative fines shall, depending on the circumstances of each individual case, be imposed in addition to, or instead of, measures referred to in points (a) to (h) and (j) of Article 58(2). When deciding whether to impose an administrative fine and deciding on the amount of the administrative fine in each individual case, due regard shall be given to the following:

    a. the nature, gravity and duration of the infringement taking into account the nature scope or purpose of the processing concerned as well as the number of data subjects affected and the level of damage suffered by them;

    b. the intentional or negligent character of the infringement;

    c. any action taken by the controller or processor to mitigate the damage suffered by data subjects;

    d. the degree of responsibility of the controller or processor taking into account technical and organisational measures implemented by them pursuant to Articles 25 and 32;

    e. any relevant previous infringements by the controller or processor;

8

f.   the degree of cooperation with the supervisory authority, in order to remedy the infringement and mitigate the possible adverse effects of the infringement;

g.   the categories of personal data affected by the infringement;

h.   the manner in which the infringement became known to the supervisory authority, in particular whether, and if so to what extent, the controller or processor notified the infringement;

i.   where measures referred to in Article 58(2) have previously been ordered against the controller or processor concerned with regard to the same subject-matter, compliance with those measures;

j.   adherence to approved codes of conduct pursuant to Article 40 or approved certification mechanisms pursuant to Article 42; and

k.   any other aggravating or mitigating factor applicable to the circumstances of the case, such as financial benefits gained, or losses avoided, directly or indirectly, from the infringement.

3.   If a controller or processor intentionally or negligently, for the same or linked processing operations, infringes several provisions of this Regulation, the total amount of the administrative fine shall not exceed the amount specified for the gravest infringement.

4.   Infringements of the following provisions shall, in accordance with paragraph 2, be subject to administrative fines up to 10,000,000 EUR, or in the case of an undertaking, up to 2% of the total worldwide annual turnover of the preceding financial year, whichever is higher:

a. the obligations of the controller and the processor pursuant to Articles 8, 11, 25 to 39 and 42 and 43;

b. the obligations of the certification body pursuant to Articles 42 and 43;

c. the obligations of the monitoring body pursuant to Article 41(4).

5. Infringements of the following provisions shall, in accordance with paragraph 2, be subject to administrative fines up to 20,000,000 EUR, or in the case of an undertaking, up to 4% of the total worldwide annual turnover of the preceding financial year, whichever is higher:

a. the basic principles for processing, including conditions for consent, pursuant to Articles 5, 6, 7 and 9;

b. the data subjects' rights pursuant to Articles 12 to 22;

c. the transfers of personal data to a recipient in a third country or an international organisation pursuant to Articles 44 to 49;

d. any obligations pursuant to Member State law adopted under Chapter IX;

e. non-compliance with an order or a temporary or definitive limitation on processing or the suspension of data flows by the supervisory authority pursuant to Article 58(2) or failure to provide access in violation of Article 58(1).

6. Non-compliance with an order by the supervisory authority as referred to in Article 58(2) shall, in accordance with paragraph 2 of this Article, be subject to administrative fines up to 20,000,000 EUR, or in the case of an undertaking, up to 4% of the total worldwide annual turnover of the preceding financial year, whichever is higher.

8

7. Without prejudice to the corrective powers of supervisory authorities pursuant to Article 58(2), each Member State may lay down the rules on whether and to what extent administrative fines may be imposed on public authorities and bodies established in that Member State.

8. The exercise by the supervisory authority of its powers under this Article shall be subject to appropriate procedural safeguards in accordance with Union and Member State law, including effective judicial remedy and due process.

9. Where the legal system of the Member State does not provide for administrative fines, this Article may be applied in such a manner that the fine is initiated by the competent supervisory authority and imposed by competent national courts, while ensuring that those legal remedies are effective and have an equivalent effect to the administrative fines imposed by supervisory authorities. In any event, the fines imposed shall be effective, proportionate and dissuasive. Those Member States shall notify to the Commission the provisions of their laws which they adopt pursuant to this paragraph by 25 May 2018 and, without delay, any subsequent amendment law or amendment affecting them.

Easy Peasy Summary

Fines can be imposed separately or alongside other measures ...

- Supervisory authorities must make sure that fines are effective, proportional, and deterrent.

- Fines can be imposed separately or alongside any other measures (listed in Article 58).

- When deciding whether to impose a fine and how much to set it at, the following should be considered:

- the nature and seriousness (including its purpose, scale, and impact on affected individuals);

- intention or negligence;

- actions taken to minimise damage;

- responsibility level (given any technical and organisational measures taken);

- previous offences;

- cooperation with the supervisory authority;

- categories of data affected;

- notification of the infringement;

- compliance with previously ordered measures;

- adherence to code of conduct or certification mechanism; and

- any other relevant factors.

- If a controller or processor intentionally or negligently violates multiple provisions of this Regulation for the same or related processing activities, the total amount of fines should not exceed the amount set for the most serious violation.

- For violations of:

  - Article 8;

  - Article 11;

  - Articles 25 to 39;

  - Article 42; and

  - Article 43,

  fines can be <u>up to 10 million EUR or 2% of the total annual global revenue</u> (whichever is higher).

8

- For infringements of:

  - Article 5;

  - Article 6;

  - Article 7;

  - Article 9;

  - Articles 12 to 22;

  - Articles 44 to 49; and

  - Article 58,

  fines can be <u>up to 20 million EUR or 4% of the total annual global revenue</u> (whichever is higher).

- Each Member State can decide whether and to what extent fines can be imposed on its public authorities and bodies.

- Member States must inform the Commission of new laws imposing these fines, and any subsequent amendments.

- The supervisory authority must be subject to appropriate procedures, including effective judicial remedies and fairness.

Article 84
Penalties

Official GDPR Text

1. Member States shall lay down the rules on other penalties applicable to infringements of this Regulation in particular for infringements which are not subject to administrative fines pursuant to Article 83, and shall take all measures necessary to ensure that they are implemented.

2. Such penalties shall be effective, proportionate and dissuasive.

3. Each Member State shall notify to the Commission the provisions of its law which it adopts pursuant to paragraph 1, by 25 May 2018 and, without delay, any subsequent amendment affecting them.

Easy Peasy Summary

- Member States must establish punishments for violations of this Regulation, especially those that cannot be fined.

- Necessary steps must be taken to ensure these penalties are enforced.

- Penalties should effectively discourage future violations and be suitable for the offense.

- Member States must inform the Commission of any new laws and amendments and should provide any further updates without delay.

Necessary steps must be taken to ensure these penalties are enforced.

8

9

Provisions Relating to Specific Processing Situations

Article 85

Processing and Freedom of Expression and Information

Official GDPR Text

1. Member States shall by law reconcile the right to the protection of personal data pursuant to this Regulation with the right to freedom of expression and information, including processing for journalistic purposes and the purposes of academic, artistic or literary expression.

2. For processing carried out for journalistic purposes or the purpose of academic artistic or literary expression, Member States shall provide for exemptions or derogations from Chapter II (principles), Chapter III (rights of the data subject), Chapter IV (controller and processor), Chapter V (transfer of personal data to third countries or international organisations), Chapter VI (independent supervisory authorities), Chapter VII (cooperation and consistency) and Chapter IX (specific data processing situations) if they are necessary to reconcile the right to the protection of personal data with the freedom of expression and information.

3. Each Member State shall notify to the Commission the provisions of its law which it has adopted pursuant to paragraph 2 and, without delay, any subsequent amendment law or amendment affecting them.

Easy Peasy Summary

- Member States must make sure that the right to personal data protection is balanced with the right to freedom of expression and information.

- Member States should provide exemptions for processing carried out for:

  o journalistic;

  o academic;

  o artistic; or

  o literary expression.

- Each Member State must notify the Commission of their adopted provisions and any other changes.

... must notify the Commission of their adopted provisions ...

9

Article 86

Processing and Public Access to Official Documents

Official GDPR Text

Personal data in official documents held by a public authority or a public body or a private body for the performance of a task carried out in the public interest may be disclosed by the authority or body in accordance with Union or Member State law to which the public authority or body is subject, in order to reconcile public access to official documents with the right to the protection of personal data pursuant to this Regulation.

Easy Peasy Summary

- Public or private bodies holding personal data in official documents for public interest tasks can disclose it according to Union or Member State laws.

- This is to balance public access and personal data protection under this Regulation.

Article 87

Processing of the National Identification Number

Official GDPR Text

Member States may further determine the specific conditions for the processing of a national identification number or any other identifier of general application. In that case the national identification number or any other identifier of general application shall be used only under appropriate safeguards for the rights and freedoms of the data subject pursuant to this Regulation.

Easy Peasy Summary

Member States can set conditions for processing national identification numbers or other general identifiers, but only with appropriate safeguards to protect the data subject's rights and freedoms under this Regulation.

9

Article 88

Processing in the Context of Employment

Official GDPR Text

1. Member States may, by law or by collective agreements, provide for more specific rules to ensure the protection of the rights and freedoms in respect of the processing of employees' personal data in the employment context, in particular for the purposes of the recruitment, the performance of the contract of employment, including discharge of obligations laid down by law or by collective agreements, management, planning and organisation of work, equality and diversity in the workplace, health and safety at work, protection of employer's or customer's property and for the purposes of the exercise and enjoyment, on an individual or collective basis, of rights and benefits related to employment, and for the purpose of the termination of the employment relationship.

2. Those rules shall include suitable and specific measures to safeguard the data subject's human dignity, legitimate interests and fundamental rights, with particular regard to the transparency of processing, the transfer of personal data within a group of undertakings, or a group of enterprises engaged in a joint economic activity and monitoring systems at the work place.

3. Each Member State shall notify to the Commission those provisions of its law which it adopts pursuant to paragraph 1, by 25 May 2018 and, without delay, any subsequent amendment affecting them.

Easy Peasy Summary

- Member States have the authority to create laws and collective agreements that protect employee personal data.

- These rules apply to:

  o recruitment;

  o contract performance;

  o work management;

  o diversity and equality at the workplace;

  o health and safety at work;

  o employer/customer property protection;

  o employment-related rights and benefits; and

  o termination of employment.

- Rules must be in place to protect:

  o employee rights and dignity;

  o their interests and fundamental rights;

  o transparency of processing;

  o data sharing within a group of related businesses; and

  o monitoring systems at the workplace.

- Each Member State must notify the Commission of their adopted provisions and any subsequent amendments.

Rules must be in place to protect employee rights and dignity ...

9

Article 89

Safeguards and Derogations Relating to Processing for Archiving Purposes in the Public Interest, Scientific or Historical Research Purposes or Statistical Purposes

Official GDPR Text

1. Processing for archiving purposes in the public interest, scientific or historical research purposes or statistical purposes, shall be subject to appropriate safeguards, in accordance with this Regulation, for the rights and freedoms of the data subject. Those safeguards shall ensure that technical and organisational measures are in place in particular in order to ensure respect for the principle of data minimisation. Those measures may include pseudonymisation provided that those purposes can be fulfilled in that manner. Where those purposes can be fulfilled by further processing which does not permit or no longer permits the identification of data subjects, those purposes shall be fulfilled in that manner.

2. Where personal data are processed for scientific or historical research purposes or statistical purposes, Union or Member State law may provide for derogations from the rights referred to in Articles 15, 16, 18 and 21 subject to the conditions and safeguards referred to in paragraph 1 of this Article in so far as such rights are likely to render impossible or seriously impair the achievement of the specific purposes, and such derogations are necessary for the fulfilment of those purposes.

3. Where personal data are processed for archiving purposes in the public interest, Union or Member State law may provide for derogations from the rights referred to in Articles 15, 16, 18, 19, 20 and 21 subject to the conditions and safeguards referred to in paragraph 1 of this Article in so far as such rights are likely to render impossible or seriously impair the achievement of the specific purposes, and such derogations are necessary for the fulfilment of those purposes.

4. Where processing referred to in paragraphs 2 and 3 serves at the same time another purpose, the derogations shall apply only to processing for the purposes referred to in those paragraphs.

Easy Peasy Summary

- Processing for archiving purposes in the public interest, scientific or historical research or statistical purposes must have appropriate safeguards in place.

- These safeguards should include measures such as data minimisation, pseudonymisation, and anonymisation.

- Union or Member State law can provide exceptions to the rights of data subject in Articles 15, 16, 18 and 21, and additionally, Articles 19 and 20 (only for archiving purposes in public interest), when processing personal data for:

  o scientific;

  o historical research;

  o statistical purposes; or

  o archiving purposes in the public interest.

- These exceptions are only applicable if they:

  o are necessary to achieve the specific purpose; and

  o would otherwise make it impossible or seriously impair it.

... safeguards should include measures such as data minimisation ...

9

253

Article 90
Obligations of Secrecy

Official GDPR Text

1. Member States may adopt specific rules to set out the powers of the supervisory authorities laid down in points (e) and (f) of Article 58(1) in relation to controllers or processors that are subject, under Union or Member State law or rules established by national competent bodies, to an obligation of professional secrecy or other equivalent obligations of secrecy where this is necessary and proportionate to reconcile the right of the protection of personal data with the obligation of secrecy. Those rules shall apply only with regard to personal data which the controller or processor has received as a result of or has obtained in an activity covered by that obligation of secrecy.

2. Each Member State shall notify to the Commission the rules adopted pursuant to paragraph 1, by 25 May 2018 and, without delay, any subsequent amendment affecting them.

Easy Peasy Summary

*   Member States can set specific rules that balance the right of protection of personal data with obligations of secrecy.

*   These rules will only apply when the controller or processor has received or obtained the personal data through an activity covered by said obligation of secrecy.

Article 91

Existing Data Protection Rules of Churches and Religious Associations

Official GDPR Text

1. Where in a Member State, churches and religious associations or communities apply, at the time of entry into force of this Regulation, comprehensive rules relating to the protection of natural persons with regard to processing, such rules may continue to apply, provided that they are brought into line with this Regulation.

2. Churches and religious associations which apply comprehensive rules in accordance with paragraph 1 of this Article shall be subject to the supervision of an independent supervisory authority, which may be specific, provided that it fulfils the conditions laid down in Chapter VI of this Regulation.

Easy Peasy Summary

- Churches and religious associations or communities can continue to apply their existing rules for processing, as long as those rules align with this Regulation.

- Churches and religious associations with comprehensive rules must be monitored by an independent supervisory authority,

Churches and religious associations ... must be monitored by an independent supervisory authority.

9

10

Delegated Acts and Implementing Acts

Article 92

Exercise of the Delegation

Official GDPR Text

1. The power to adopt delegated acts is conferred on the Commission subject to the conditions laid down in this Article.

2. The delegation of power referred to in Article 12(8) and Article 43(8) shall be conferred on the Commission for an indeterminate period of time from 24 May 2016.

3. The delegation of power referred to in Article 12(8) and Article 43(8) may be revoked at any time by the European Parliament or by the Council. A decision of revocation shall put an end to the delegation of power specified in that decision. It shall take effect the day following that of its publication in the Official Journal of the European Union or at a later date specified therein. It shall not affect the validity of any delegated acts already in force.

4. As soon as it adopts a delegated act, the Commission shall notify it simultaneously to the European Parliament and to the Council.

5. A delegated act adopted pursuant to Article 12(8) and Article 43(8) shall enter into force only if no objection has been expressed by either the European Parliament or the Council within a period of three months of notification of that act to the European Parliament and the Council or if, before the expiry of that period, the European Parliament and the Council have both informed the Commission that they will not object. That period shall be extended by three months at the initiative of the European Parliament or of the Council.

Easy Peasy Summary

- The Commission has authority to issue delegated acts, subject to the conditions outlined in this Article.

- The Commission has this authority with no expiry date.

- The European Parliament or Council can revoke the delegated power at any time.

- Such a decision will end the delegation and take effect the day after it is published in the Official Journal of the European Union or later.

- Such a decision will not affect existing delegated acts.

- Once the Commission adopts a delegated act, it must immediately notify the European Parliament and the Council.

- A delegated act from Article 12(8) and Article 43(8) becomes effective if, within 3 months, the European Parliament and the Council do not object or inform the Commission they will not object. This 3-month period can be extended by another 3 months if necessary.

The Commission has this authority with no expiry date.

10

Article 93

Committee Procedure

Official GDPR Text

1. The Commission shall be assisted by a committee. That committee shall be a committee within the meaning of Regulation (EU) No 182/2011.

2. Where reference is made to this paragraph, Article 5 of Regulation (EU) No 182/2011 shall apply.

3. Where reference is made to this paragraph, Article 8 of Regulation ((EU) No 182/2011, in conjunction with Article 5 thereof, shall apply.

The Commission will have a Committee for assistance.

Easy Peasy Summary

•   The Commission will have a Committee for assistance.

•   References to 'Committee' in Regulation (EU) No 182/2011 means this Committee.

11

Final Provisions

Article 94
Repeal of Directive 95/46/EC

Official GDPR Text

1. Directive 95/46/EC is repealed with effect from 25 May 2018.

2. References to the repealed Directive shall be construed as references to this Regulation. References to the Working Party on the Protection of Individuals with regard to the Processing of Personal Data established by Article 29 of Directive 95/46/EC shall be construed as references to the European Data Protection Board established by this Regulation.

Easy Peasy Summary

- Directive 95/46/EC has been repealed as of 25 May 2018.

- All references to the Directive shall be understood to mean this Regulation. Any references to the Article 29 Working Party will now be regarded as references to the European Data Protection Board.

Article 95

Relationship With Directive 2002/58/EC

Official GDPR Text

This Regulation shall not impose additional obligations on natural or legal persons in relation to processing in connection with the provision of publicly available electronic communications services in public communication networks in the Union in relation to matters for which they are subject to specific obligations with the same objective set out in Directive 2002/58/EC.

Easy Peasy Summary

This Regulation does not add extra duties for individuals or companies processing publicly available electronic communications services in public networks, if they already have specific obligations with the same goal under Directive 2002/58/EC.

11

Article 96

Relationship With Previously Concluded Agreements

Official GDPR Text

International agreements involving the transfer of personal data to third countries or international organisations which were concluded by Member States prior to 24 May 2016, and which comply with Union law as applicable prior to that date, shall remain in force until amended, replaced or revoked.

Easy Peasy Summary

Previous international agreements made by Member States before 24 May 2016 that follow Union law from before that date regarding the transfer of personal data to third countries or international organisations will continue until changed, substituted, or cancelled.

Article 97

Commission Reports

Official GDPR Text

1. By 25 May 2020 and every four years thereafter, the Commission shall submit a report on the evaluation and review of this Regulation to the European Parliament and to the Council. The reports shall be made public.

2. In the context of the evaluations and reviews referred to in paragraph 1, the Commission shall examine, in particular, the application and functioning of:

    a. Chapter V on the transfer of personal data to third countries or international organisations with particular regard to decisions adopted pursuant to Article 45(3) of this Regulation and decisions adopted on the basis of Article 25(6) of Directive 95/46/EC;

    b. Chapter VII on cooperation and consistency.

3. For the purpose of paragraph 1, the Commission may request information from Member States and supervisory authorities.

4. In carrying out the evaluations and reviews referred to in paragraphs 1 and 2, the Commission shall take into account the positions and findings of the European Parliament, of the Council, and of other relevant bodies or sources.

5. The Commission shall, if necessary, submit appropriate proposals to amend this Regulation, in particular taking into account of developments in information technology and in the light of the state of progress in the information society.

11

Easy Peasy Summary

- Every four years starting from 25 May 2020, the Commission will present a public report on the assessment and review of this Regulation to both the European Parliament and Council.

- When carrying out the evaluations and reviews, the Commission should consider the positions and findings of the European Parliament, Council, and other relevant sources.

- The Commission can ask for information from Member States and supervisory authorities for compiling the reports.

- During the evaluations and reviews, the Commission will specifically investigate Chapter V's operation on transferring personal data to third countries or international organisations as well as Chapter VII's cooperation and consistency.

The reports should be made public.

- The reports should be made public.

- The Commission can submit proposals to make changes to this Regulation based on developments in information technology and the progress of the information society if necessary.

Article 98

Review of Other Union Legal Acts on Data Protection

Official GDPR Text

The Commission shall, if appropriate, submit legislative proposals with a view to amending other Union legal acts on the protection of personal data, in order to ensure uniform and consistent protection of natural persons with regard to processing. This shall in particular concern the rules relating to the protection of natural persons with regard to processing by Union institutions, bodies, offices and agencies and on the free movement of such data.

Easy Peasy Summary

- The Commission can propose changes to other Union legal acts on personal data protection, if necessary, to ensure consistent and uniform protection for individuals during processing.

- This includes rules related to protecting individuals when Union institutions or agencies process their data, as well as the free movement of that data.

11

Article 99

Entry Into Force and Application

Official GDPR Text

1. This Regulation shall enter into force on the twentieth day following that of its publication in the Official Journal of the European Union.

2. It shall apply from 25 May 2018.

Easy Peasy Summary

The Regulation is effective from 25 May 2018.

Next Steps...

5 FREE Resources to Unlock
More Data Privacy Insights and
Join the Community of Thriving Privacy Pros

You've just finished reading *The Easy Peasy Guide to GDPR*, and it has given you greater clarity, more confidence, and been a transformative experience for you.

But don't stop there!

As a privacy professional, continuous learning and networking are essential for staying ahead in this rapidly evolving field.

That's why I invite you to connect with me and become part of my thriving community.

1. Watch the Privacy Pros YouTube Channel

Get access to exclusive video content, where I share my extensive knowledge, practical tips and insights on data privacy, industry trends and rapid career growth secrets. Plus, you'll be the first to know when new videos are released.

Don't miss out on these valuable learning opportunities!

Get insights here: https://www.youtube.com/@PrivacyPros

2. Tune in to the Privacy Pros Podcast

Stay informed and inspired by tuning in to the Privacy Pros Podcast. I interview leading experts and thought leaders in the data privacy field.

You'll gain insights into their experiences, success stories and challenges, helping you grow both personally and professionally.

Get inspired here: https://privacypros.captivate.fm/listen

3. Join my Facebook Group: Privacy Pros Academy

Become a part of our engaged and supportive Facebook community, where you can share your thoughts, ask questions and connect with fellow data privacy professionals.

You'll also receive regular updates on the latest news, events and resources to help you excel in your career.

Become part of the community here: https://www.facebook.com/privacypros

4. Connect with me on LinkedIn

Grow your professional network by connecting with me on LinkedIn.

You'll have the opportunity to engage in thought-provoking discussions, stay updated on the latest data privacy trends, and connect with other like-minded professionals in the field.

Your network is your net worth.

Connect with me here: https://www.linkedin.com/in/kmjahmed/

5. Subscribe to the Privacy Pros Newsletter

Stay in the loop and never miss an update with the Privacy Pros Newsletter!

Receive the latest news, tips and best practices in the world of data privacy, delivered straight to your inbox. With expert insights and exclusive content, this newsletter is your one-stop source for staying ahead in the ever-evolving data privacy landscape.

Get ahead here: https://newsletter.privacypros.academy/sign-up

Don't miss out on these incredible opportunities to connect, grow and thrive alongside fellow data privacy professionals from around the globe.

I'm excited to have you as a part of our thriving community, and look forward to empowering you on your journey towards data privacy excellence.

Become a World Class Privacy Leader & Future Proof Your Career

Embark on a transformative journey and elevate your data privacy career with our industry-leading mentoring programs, designed to provide you with the knowledge, skills and confidence you need to excel from Privacy Pros Academy.

Privacy Pros Accelerator Program

Kick-start your data privacy career with our Privacy Pros Accelerator Program, a holistic and comprehensive mentoring experience tailored to help you navigate the complex world of data privacy.

Learn from the best and gain the mindset for success, develop subject matter expertise, build your personal brand, enhance your leadership and management abilities, and master practical skills.

Apply to join the Privacy Pros Accelerator Program here: https://calendly.com/privacypros/apply

The Ultimate CIPP/E Certification Program for High Performance Professionals

Master the essentials of European data protection with our Ultimate CIPP/E Certification Program for High-Performance Professionals.

This mentoring program will guide you through the entire process, from understanding GDPR to passing the certification exam, ensuring that you're fully equipped to tackle European privacy challenges.

Apply to join the Ultimate CIPP/E Certification Program for High-Performance Professionals here: https://calendly.com/privacypros/apply

The Ultimate CIPM Certification Program for Privacy Leaders

Become a certified privacy management expert with our Ultimate CIPM Certification Program for Privacy Leaders.

This comprehensive program offers an in-depth understanding of privacy program management, equipping you with the skills needed to operationalise, implement and maintain a robust privacy program.

Apply to join the Ultimate CIPM Certification Program for Privacy Leaders here:

https://calendly.com/privacypros/apply

The Ultimate CIPT Certification Program for Privacy Futurists

Embrace the future of data privacy with our Ultimate CIPT Certification Program for Privacy Futurists.

Discover how to navigate the intersection of privacy and technology, build privacy by design, and become an invaluable asset to any organisation in the rapidly evolving privacy landscape.

Apply to join the Ultimate CIPT Certification Program for Privacy Futurists here: https://calendly.com/privacypros/apply

Take advantage of these unparalleled mentoring opportunities and propel your data privacy career to new heights.

Under my guidance, you'll gain the expertise, confidence and support necessary to make a lasting impact in the world of data privacy.

Get Your Business GDPR Compliant, Protect Your Reputation & Attract More Clients

Unlock the Power of Privacy with award-winning pragmatic solutions from Kazient Privacy Experts.

Privacy Consultancy

Stay ahead of the curve with our expert privacy consultancy services.

We'll help your business navigate the complex world of data privacy regulations, develop robust privacy programs, and minimise risk while maximizing growth in a language everyone can understand.

DPIA Services

Ensure your projects and processes are compliant with our specialized DPIA services.

Our team of experts will conduct thorough assessments, identify potential risks, and develop tailored mitigation strategies to protect your organisation and customers.

Data Protection Officer (DPO) as a Service

Outsource your DPO responsibilities to our seasoned professionals, who have the experience and knowledge to safeguard your organisation's data privacy.

We'll ensure compliance, manage risks, and handle all aspects of data protection on your behalf.

Data Privacy Training & Workshops

Equip your team with the necessary skills and knowledge to excel in the rapidly evolving privacy landscape.

Our dynamic training sessions and interactive workshops cover essential topics, such as GDPR, international transfers, data subject requests, and so much more – ensuring your team is always one step ahead.

Partner with us for your data privacy challenges to gain a trusted ally in the ever-changing world of data privacy.

Don't miss out on the opportunity to secure your organisation's future – get in touch with us today to learn more about our comprehensive and pragmatic solutions.

Protect your business here: https://calendly.com/privacypro/discovery-call

About the Author

Jamal Ahmed, the "King of Data Protection" as dubbed by the BBC, is not just the reigning global expert on data privacy – he is a passionate advocate for privacy rights. His commitment to ensuring that organisations treat personal data with the utmost respect and earn the trust of their customers sets him apart as a leader in the field of data privacy and protection.

With a reputation for providing pragmatic and easy-to-implement solutions for governments, SMEs and publicly listed multinational corporations including PwC, Deloitte, EY, KPMG, UBS, Vodafone and Meta, Jamal is dedicated to helping clients achieve compliance with global privacy regulations across a vast range of sectors.

He is a trusted media commentator and appears regularly on BBC News, ITV News, Sky News and other prestigious international television channels, as well as on radio stations including BBC Worldwide, talkRadio and LBC. Jamal's expertise has been featured in numerous globally renowned publications such as *The Independent*, *The Guardian*, *MSN*, *RTE*, *Foreign Policy* and *Euronews*.

Jamal's signature "Easy Peasy" style of delivery has made him one of the most sought-after keynote speakers in the industry. His passion for privacy, coupled with his talent to break down complex topics into clear, concise and actionable insights, has captured and engaged audiences of all backgrounds and expertise levels around the globe.

Ranked #1 in the world, his *Privacy Pros* podcast has become a staple for privacy professionals in 117 countries and counting. Featuring the brightest minds in the industry, it is the go-to source for expert insights and advice.

Jamal and his award-winning consultancy **Kazient Privacy Experts**, based in the City of London, is at the forefront of the data privacy industry. His premier mentoring platform, *Privacy Pros Academy*, is setting the standard for data privacy education. He's earned recognition for excellence including *Best Data Protection & GDPR Consultants*, *Excellence in Enterprise*, and *Best Data Privacy Training Provider*.

If you're looking for a data privacy and protection expert who can provide a complete solution for all your needs, Jamal Ahmed, the *King of Data Protection*, is the name you need to remember. With years of experience and a deep understanding of privacy rights, he can guide you through the complexities of data privacy. Jamal can help you build a culture that prioritises privacy, sets you apart, and earns the trust of your customers.

https://kazient.co.uk

facebook.com/privacyexperts

Twitter: @KazientPrivacy   @JamalPrivacyPro

linkedin.com/in/kmjahmed

Instagram: @privacyexperts

Ingram Content Group UK Ltd.
Milton Keynes UK
UKHW030818200723
425492UK00009B/444